HOW TO TA.... ANYONE LIKE YOU'RE AN EXTROVERT

DISCOVER THE SECRETS TO TALKING CONFIDENTLY AND NATURALLY TO FRIENDS, FAMILY, WORKMATES, AND EVEN STRANGERS

SOCIAL IQ ACADEMY

CONTENTS

INTRODUCTION

Introduction

The 70-year-old family business was facing a serious crisis due to competition and wrong decisions made by the CEO who was in charge for the last twenty years. The business climate was not good at the company, with cost cuts, lay-offs, and a high level of uncertainty and anxiety that affected everybody. John, the 32-year-old marketing director, was named for the CEO position. It was a big and stressful challenge, mainly because although he was a director, his uncle, the old CEO, never delegated real important tasks to him.

John felt quite insecure about making decisions and maintaining control. So, he did the next best thing: he sought the help of a big consulting company that had served the company for a long time. On the same day, three experienced consultants were there, helping him make a complete diagnosis of the situation—and giving him much needed security.

At the end of the second day of exhaustive analyses, talking to leaders, reading reports, and meetings, the consultants went to John's office. The young executive honestly asked them, "What does the situation look like? I am not prepared for the challenge because I was the marketing director, but my uncle did not delegate important things to me. I am confused and want you to tell me what I should do."

The consultants answered, "Simply take care of communication. Through your body language, words, and commitment to working with your staff and your partners, you will transmit peace of mind to everyone. Just talk to people and exchange ideas. The machinery will work efficiently because the company has all the conditions to overcome this crisis, and your staff knows exactly what to do."

Five years later at a meeting of businesspeople, John, the now experienced CEO, said: "It was the wisest advice I ever received. When you have a problem of any nature, rely on communication as the path to a solution."

That's it. There is no novelty here. What do leaders do? They talk all the time according to many studies I have read from the 1980s until now.[1,2] They do not have time to read, ponder over plans, reflect freely without interruptions, or make complex calculations. They just talk to negotiate, solve conflicts, motivate people, clarify strategies, brainstorm, and sell ideas. As a professor, I always put my MBA students in front of the class to present projects, and explain to them that leadership is mostly focused on oral communication.

Do you want to engage your team, encourage cooperation, reduce stress in the workplace, create a dream team, and establish a supportive network within and without the organization? Improve your communication. Do you want to grow, do more for your organization, and achieve success? Improve your conversation skills.

In fact, do you have any problems at work, in your family, or social life? Use your conversation toolkit because most probably the solution will be a good conversation, or at least it will be a great part of the solution. Well-developed conversation skills make you more productive, less stressed, and happier.

That's the theme of this book. It will discuss all the main aspects of personal communication, such as reading other people, cultivating the right attitudes, developing empathy, being alert about body language, and using your body to strengthen your messages. In summary, it will present information and ideas that can help you become an excellent communicator. If you want, the magic will happen.

I have worked as a consultant, Master's in Business Administration (MBA) professor, and trainer for the last five decades, observing organizational, business, and career dynamics. I interact with frontline workers, entry-level professionals, executives, and top executives, with special interest in business and communication, the areas of my master's and PhD degrees, respectively. I bring my readings and observations to discuss with you. It is not simply a book of techniques, but an invitation to sincere reflection that I hope can change your life.

What are your biggest problems and objectives today? Use your conversation toolkit, and the solutions will come. I hope to help you in this journey.

José Antônio Rosa

PhD. in Communication Sciences

THE MAGIC OF CONVERSATION

HOW CAN YOU HARNESS THE POWER OF SPEECH TO BECOME MORE LOVED, INFLUENTIAL, PRODUCTIVE, AND HAPPY?

Growing up, I was a serious and reflective boy, with little interest in playing with the gang. My preference was to stay at home or in other places where adults talked about their lives and everyday matters. One of my favorite speakers was my dad, the mayor of the small city where we lived.

One day, there was a failure in the water supply service in the city, and the entire population was temporarily without water. You know, in a small town, every inconvenience is the mayor's fault, from a meteor crash to a kid showing up with stinky feet. So, my father was to blame for the lack of water in the citizens' homes.

On that complicated day, he and I were at the door of the house when we saw that, in the distance, a VIP was coming towards us, furious and unwashed. It was Alice, a successful and easily agitated merchant, who everyone feared, because she makes scandals and people hate them.

"Whoa," I said to Dad, "I swear she is coming to kill you because of the water. How do we get outta here scot-free?"

"Well," he replied, "with the only effective and possible way for the moment: with a good conversation."

Then, the beast arrived, with no "good morning," no "hi, folks," no good conversation opener. She attacked the problem directly with a high, furious voice. After hearing thirty or forty sentences, my father invited her to enter and take a seat.

My father just listened calmly with a caring expression, looking into her eyes. As the conversation progressed, she became calmer, more understanding, and more friendly. One hour after the beast's arrival, a sweet and smiling beauty left our house. Still unwashed, but happy.

I later told my father that I swore he wouldn't be able to handle that stormy encounter. He replied, "It was easy-peasy, son. I'm good at it. That's why I am the mayor."

The main lesson I learned from this episode is that good conversation solves problems, improves people's understanding, and makes people happier.

So, want to have fun? Want to get along in the best way with other people? Want to solve your problems and help people solve theirs? Want to contribute to social peace? Want to lead and become your city's mayor? In short, do you want to grow in your social and professional life and increase your potential for success and happiness? Become skilled in interpersonal communications by studying, observing, and doing. Each challenge you overcome in practicing will bring a great return.

What Conversation Really Is

Defined in the simplest way, conversation is a sequential exchange of information, a turn-taking process.[1] As a guideline, be careful with your turns and respect others when talking. Many people these days are very eager to talk but unwilling to listen.

As "all men seek one goal: success or happiness," as posited by Aristotle,[2] conversation is a goal-oriented process where people try just to have fun or to share information, build rapport, or persuade each other.

As conversation is a human process, objective rationality is just one aspect, but emotions are always involved.[3] Saying a "smiling hello" to the mailman makes you and them feel good. The emotional burden in conversations can vary greatly from situation to situation: from almost zero to a heart attack.

Your words can anger, disappoint, alienate, or sadden someone. Alternatively, you can and should also improve a person's self-esteem, self-confidence, optimism, and trust in life and in others; in short, you can improve people's happiness.

Two questions for you:

- What was Alice's goal?
- Why did father give her such a long first turn in the conversation?

During that time, I tried to guess it. Maybe Alice just wanted to scold someone to calm her fury. I knew something for sure: there were strong emotions involved. Now, I know that my wise father realized her goal, and I also understand why he gave her such a long turn in the conversation. She certainly wanted to pressure my father to solve the problem, but mostly she wanted to talk, because talking heals our wounds.

That's why, in all societies, ways were developed to let people talk. For example, religions usually have confessions in their traditions. There is also the Wailing Wall. Freudian psychotherapy, based on structured conversation, became known appropriately as the "talking cure".[4] By allowing her time to speak, Dad let Alice calm down, control her emotions, and cure herself for the conversation to be successful.

The idea of talking cure brings quite a very important point, I want to share an experience with you:

During the end of the 1990s and beginning of the 2000s, I worked for a human resources (HR) consulting firm. At that time, many companies were downsizing, which meant there were mass layoffs. Many of these companies offered support to the laid off people for career continuation, and I was part of a team that provided training for these people shortly after they were laid off.

Guess what the first part of the training event was? It was asking people to talk about their history, situation, and future. In that process, they understood their situation better, recovered part of their broken self-esteem and self-confidence, and acquired a glimmer of hope. I learned that it works very well for all kinds of groups: blue and white-collar, from different areas, regions, and ages.

One more important observation about what conversation is: when two people are involved in a dialog, in fact, there are more than two "people" on stage. Why? People have roles to play in their social lives. Conversation is always a role-playing process, which means it is impossible just to be yourself because your role will be present and influence the process.[5] Roles are sets of social expectations and rules we must adhere to in different social contexts to function effectively. Each person has many roles and personas expected to behave accordingly.

Dad was not just himself when talking to Alice. He was first and foremost the mayor, because that was the persona she came to see. He was also her friend, a man, and my dad (because I was there, watching the fight). Alice was a frustrated citizen, a friend, and a woman.

Even I, who was just observing, had my role as a curious son to respect. For example, I couldn't take part, talk, or bother them.

Here's the last observation about conversation for now: It is a powerful tool humans use to build "reality," which means it is a process where people jointly construct meaning.[6] The result is reality—things as we see them socially, and also our singular view—things as we see them individually. It includes big metaphysical subjects: the purpose of life, who we are, and what is next. It also includes things pertaining to our daily lives: the role of the mayor, who Alice is, whether the boy should hear the conversation.

Provocative questions for you:

- Who do you think you are? How many contributions from other people are included in your self-image?
- How many years does it take a person to get rid of a painful self-image that their parents "constructed"?
- How much of the image of person X or Y is just a perception created by you?

Have you ever asked other people who you really are in their eyes? We often don't want to know and prefer to maintain our illusory self-concepts. Or we are often embarrassed to ask. Both situations result in barriers to our complete self-knowledge and growth. Remember the ancient advice from the Oracle of Delphi, given by Socrates as one of the first steps towards personal excellence: Know yourself.

How To Talk Like A Pro

Conversation is a very complex process, isn't it? It involves people with varying skill levels, different values, emotions, roles, and momentary states. It is affected by the situation or context that brought the actors together, such as a water supply problem. And it is regulated by culture and other items of the broad environment—technology, economy, politics, laws, climate, and many more. Looking at the whole picture, it seems that we must be a mixture of artists with doctorates in Psychology to perform conversations with excellence, but it is far from this.

Remember that it is mostly a natural process, developed instinctively by humans over millennia. Therefore, the knowledge is already within you, and the mechanics of the skills are also there. You just need to reconnect with your inner master and artist. Expressed academic, common sense, and recorded knowledge will help you do this.

I asked my father what the most relevant rules for being "good at conversations" would be and researched the literature. I also added my 50 years of experience leading people, teaching, and training. The answer to "How to speak like a pro" will be endless because it is subject to lifelong learning. But to begin with, let's discuss some of the most important points below.

Authenticity

Authenticity refers to being genuine, true to yourself, and expressing thoughts and feelings in a way that is consistent with your values and beliefs.[5] The authentic person reveals himself as a human being, even when performing his role. They do not try to pretend to be someone they are not; they don't pretend to have qualities they don't possess; they abandon any type of mask; they do not worry about exposing their status or importance; and they act as equals.

On the contrary, an inauthentic person tries to hide their true inner self, wear social masks, and tell lies about their thoughts, feelings, values, and important beliefs.

You cannot be fully authentic because you have to respond to the demands of the roles.[5] But you can be aware of the role and your true self and bring as much authenticity to the dialogue as possible. You can do this by reminding interlocutors who you are outside of your role. My father reminded Alice that he was a weak, stressed

8

human being and her friend, at the same time in the role of mayor.

Connecting With Yourself And Others

Many times, people act or say things and then regret them. Why? Due to the demands of everyday life, they end up forgetting who they are, what they want, and what they seek to achieve in life. So, to do the right thing and have adequate speech, it is essential that the person be able to connect with themselves. Understanding your own thoughts, feelings, values, and beliefs—where they come from and how they affect you—is the first condition for connecting with yourself.

Ideally, in a conversation, both parties should have a clear understanding of themselves. But achieving a good level of self-knowledge is not easy. We tend to consider our thoughts, values, and beliefs as the truth, forgetting that they are the truth only for us. They are the result of social education in the family, in groups, at school, and in culture, not universal and objective concepts.

We also consider our feelings as if they were part of us and not as momentary situations that can be controlled and changed. Like a Buddhist teaching says, they are running through our minds. If we don't grab them, they will pass away, like a cloud in the sky.[7]

Finally, our own experience also teaches, but at the same time, it conditions our opinions, making us think that the right ideas are the ones we have. This is where prejudices against people, behaviors, lifestyles, and more come from.

In addition to developing self-knowledge, it is essential to understand our interlocutors, their needs, emotional states, desires, and the roles they express in dialogue.

People also differ in their communication styles. Some people are more detailed in their speech, others are more succinct; some elaborate their ideas in a longer way, others are quick; some speak more, others speak less. Ultimately, everyone has their own way of communicating. A good communicator seeks to accept each person's style and flexibly adapt to it. As Stephen Covey said, "Seek first to understand, then to be understood."[8]

Finally, we need to help others get to know themselves better, too. In conversation, for example, you can remind people about their roles, the parties' common interests, and the shared core values. Just like my father did with Alice, remembering her role as a friend. As soon as he could speak, he said, "My dear friend Alice." This helped her connect with her inner being and also achieve the greatest authenticity possible.

Be Present, Here And Now

People can be in a state of absence while doing things in life, as ancient Greek philosophers observed, and modern researchers also claim. This is not being aware of yourself, not being aware of the situation or of the presence of others, and not being able to achieve plain attention. For example, is a parent really present in their child's soccer game, emotionally and physically, or is there only the body while the mind is occupied with the shopping list? How about bumping into a dear friend in the store and not realizing you know them?

To achieve the highest levels of authenticity and effectiveness in communication, entering a state of presence or mindfulness is essential.[9] This means observing yourself, others, and the situation, abandoning disturbing ideas from the past, future, and elsewhere. It's taking control of your presence, here and now. It makes it much easier to control your emotions, gain mental clarity, and understand the relationship process.

Develop Empathy

If you really connect with the other inner being and enter a state of presence, empathy will arise; that is, you will think, feel, and see things like the interlocutor. This will be instinctively perceived by them, and a strong and natural positive response will appear. This creates a deep understanding between people. The good news is that empathy and sensitivity in general can be learned and developed. Anyone can learn to be more sensitive to the pain, needs, anxieties, and hopes of others. I meant that every person could learn to become a good person.

Practice The 3 Gs

Maintain a firm commitment to conversation excellence and to the 3 Gs: good intention, goodwill, and good manners. This means your sole focus will be on helping the dialogue process reach maximum efficiency. You will not use conversation to show power or personal importance, to show how interesting you are, to send hidden messages, nor to present veiled threats.

My father didn't react to Alice's emotional outburst, right? Instead, he just watched and let her fully express her feelings. If he had interpreted this as an attack on his personal worth or his authority as the mayor and responded in kind, the dialogue would certainly not have ended on good terms. Instead of being a reactive person who acts without thinking or like a robot who won't abandon their programming, he changes the tone and puts it on the right track, which means he acts as a transitional figure, as Covey said.[8]

Chapter Summary

- Conversation is one of the most important processes in structuring human life and society, making people capable of dealing with problems and challenges and happier as individuals and collectively.
- Excellence in conversation requires that people maintain the highest possible level of authenticity, being aware of and consistent with their own ideas, feelings, values, and beliefs. This can be achieved with an adequate level of self-knowledge and a sincere effort to fully understand others.
- It also requires people to connect with each other in a deep way, with their inner selves and that of

the interlocutors, understanding emotional mindsets, values, and interests, and being aware of the personas and social roles involved.

- To maintain control of the conversational process, you must enter the state of presence and be here and now. This allows you to observe and understand yourself and others, the objectives of each party, the situation, and the feelings involved; this will give rise to empathy.

- Conversation is a tool through which you and others construct reality as it is for us. You can be a builder of better humans and a better world and help others be the same.

- Ultimately, a good conversation is the magic formula that cures human pain. The right words can transform Alice from a hurt, angry person into a happy friend, even if the situation isn't ideal.

Action Steps

Here are some experiential exercises that can help you:

Difficult Conversation Analysis

Take a conflict situation conversation that happens at work or at home. Think about a) the roles involved, b) the emotions shown by people, and c) the actors' performances. After that, discuss with a sensible colleague or family member and draw conclusions about what could be improved in the conversation process.

Empathy Improvement Game

Take a person from your everyday relationship and list 10 things you think you know about that person's feelings and values. Make sentences like:

- They hate this or that.
- They love…
- They believe in…
- They don't want to be...

After making the list, talk to the person and ask about each item. Then, evaluate your success rate and discuss the matter with the person.

Take The Courage To Get To Know You

Let's do an experiential exercise that requires courage: choose the three most important people in your daily relationships at work and the three most important in your family. Ask them, "Tell me three things you think I am." Be emotionally prepared to listen. Then listen to the answers without commenting. You will reflect on them alone, later. Tell people that you will not comment on their responses.

Reflect deeply on the answers, considering that people are right because either you really are what they said or because socially you appear to be that. Remember that to others, you are only what you communicate. So, think about who you are and what you communicate.

2

MUCH MORE THAN BEAUTIFUL, RIGHT WORDS

LEARN THE SECRETS OF FULL COMMUNICATION TO GIVE STRENGTH TO WORDS AND BETTER COMMUNICATE WHAT YOU CANNOT SAY

There is a common mistake that many new communications students make. They tend to think that good messages will automatically produce excellent communication. No way. I propose discussing the subject based on a real-life story that one of my students told me. I will tell her story, divided into three parts, and ask you to reflect and answer some questions:

Part 1

The mother (my student) and her teenage daughter entered the doctor's office. The doctor was reading and, without lifting his head, asked them to sit down.

Part 2

As soon as mother and daughter sat down, the doctor looked at them with a neutral expression and asked, "How can I help you? What is the problem?"

"She is having some difficulty…" The mother began to respond, when she was interrupted by the doctor:

"Ma'am, are you being examined, or is she?"

"Well, actually, she is, but…" She replied before being interrupted again.

"So, I'd rather talk to her. Please wait outside," said the doctor in an authoritative voice that left no room for the mother to respond.

"Yes, sir," the mother replied, leaving the doctor's office.

<u>Part 3</u>

Less than a minute later, the doctor went to the door and called the mother back. He said, "Sorry, ma'am. I have to apologize. I didn't realize she couldn't hear nor speak. I'm quite stressed due to a medical incident I was involved in an hour ago. That's why I acted rudely. Let's give your daughter the attention and quality care she deserves."

"No problem, doctor. It is difficult for her to express her feelings and abstract ideas. I spend most of my time with her, and we manage to communicate in our own way. I can interpret her feelings and thoughts reasonably well. I will try to help you in the best way possible."

Think about this true story and then answer these questions:

- How would you evaluate the doctor's behavior in segments one, two, and three?

- What feelings are awakened in your mind in each segment?
- What are your thoughts about the doctor in each segment?
- What is your final opinion about the doctor?

You probably gave the doctor an F—in moments one and two, right? He failed on many important counts: he showed no empathy, no respect for his role, no ability to ask questions, and no respect for customers. So, you likely created negative feelings and thoughts about him in these two segments. But you also almost certainly forgave him and reversed your negative ideas and feelings about him in the third segment. For me, in the third segment, he deserves an A+. He showed his humanity, with its weaknesses and limitations, and acted with humility.

This short true story can be a good way to introduce many important communication concepts. Let's discuss four of these concepts, which are:

- Full communication
- Report
- Empathy and openness
- Active listening

Full Communication

How important is a word in the conversation? It depends. Its impact can vary from almost none to very high or even devastating. "You are a jerk!" This phrase can infuriate a person or make them laugh out loud. It depends on the elements involved in the process.

It was expressed in Harold Lasswell's 1948 communication model: the effectiveness and impact of a message depend on who says it, what is said, how it is said, to whom, and on what channel.[1] This is a very important and popular tool that has been expanded over time by other researchers and communication professionals to incorporate other elements such as context, cultural orientations, and forms of messages.

To attain excellence in relationships, one must understand and learn to navigate the total communication process, which includes verbal and nonverbal elements, but not only this.[2] A holistic approach to the process will result in improved clarity, tonified messages, adequacy, and cultural sensitivity.

How do we communicate? Whether voluntary or involuntary, we communicate in many ways. When we maintain awareness of these forms and manipulate them effectively, the result is excellent communication. Let's discuss some of those main ways of communicating:

<u>Attitudes</u>

Before any word is said, your attitude sends nonverbal signs to the interlocutor. Appropriate attitudes are essential for effective communication.

The American Psychological Association (APA), defines "attitude" as "a relatively enduring and general evaluation of an object, person, group, issue, or concept on a dimension ranging from negative to positive."[3] The attitudes influence our messages in both conscious and unconscious ways.

For example, doctors frequently develop negative attitudes toward mothers who try to guide the consultation of their children. Remember, attitude is a "general evaluation," that leads to a generalization, and attitudes lead to action. Therefore, our doctor was rude to the mother, who tried to explain her daughter's feelings.

Notice that negative or positive attitudes show up involuntarily in your verbal and nonverbal communication. So, without saying a single word, you may communicate that: a) you approve or reject a person; b) you are or are not against their ideas or actions; c) you tend to cooperate with or compete with them; etc.

Do you want to improve your conversation skills? Manage your attitudes adequately. Here are some tips on how to do it:

- Try to be conscious of your negative attitudes toward objects, persons, groups, issues, or concepts, and combat them. They make it difficult for you to get along with other people.
- Develop positive attitudes about relevant issues of your life, and about people—different lifestyles and behaviors, ideas, and opinions. This does not mean abandoning your own values, just

that you will not be armed and reactive against specific people or issues.

- Learn how to represent and act as a good actor. If this skill is manipulated with the 3 Gs (remember: good intention, goodwill, and good manners), it will be a powerful tool to create understanding and good relationships.
- Prejudices against people or groups are the worst barrier in the conversation process. In a world of inclusion and respect, they are not acceptable and negatively impact one's communication competence. Try to rid your mind of prejudices.

Now tell me: Why was the doctor in our story redeemed in the third segment? Bad attitudes were activated in segments one and two, but in segment three, good attitudes supplanted the bad. Some good attitudes were demonstrated:

- Humility: no arrogance from being a doctor, and in a natural position of power in relation to the mother.
- Honesty and openness: acceptance of human weakness and determination to be better.

Here's excellent news for anyone looking to improve their communication skills: it's possible—and much easier than people might imagine—to change a bad image and reputation. Address the situation and aim to be better. Human beings forgive; remember this.

In short, the doctor seemed to have the correct attitude, but he was in a state of absence, and under the control of his emotions. When he could not assist the girl during the consultation, he regained his presence and command of his emotions and presented himself as a good human being.

<u>Verbal Communication</u>

Thanks to words and verbal communication, we construct sophisticated societies and have developed, accumulated, and transmitted knowledge between generations. In daily life, verbal communication also plays an important role in structuring work, the learning process, negotiations, persuasion, and leadership for better productivity and happiness.[2]

If you want to improve your conversation efficiency, you must give the words and messages the necessary attention and maintain a continuous learning process for using them properly.

Content selection. What you decide to say or say unintentionally impacts the interlocutor and affects the conversation process.[4] For example, the doctor could have started the conversation with the mother by apologizing for delaying the appointment due to problems he had with a procedure. Instead, he jumped directly into the consultation process and then asked a very aggressive question. He didn't control his emotions and it was an automatic, instinctive response driven by his bad attitude towards overprotective mothers. He could have asked better: "Just a minute, please, ma'am. Let's see if she (the girl) can express that."

Some tips that may be useful are:

- Develop control over your speech and take command of it.
- If you have a chronic tendency to say toxic things, try to understand the feelings involved and seek change. If necessary, ask for professional help.
- When you are very stressed, choose silence and speak thoughtfully.
- Listen actively before speaking.
- Develop the habit of saying the kindest, most affectionate things appropriate to the situation. This is not opposed to assertiveness; you can be sweet but firm—a good combination.

Formal language versus nonformal language. Formal language is one in which we avoid subjectivity and use words, phrases, and structures appropriate to professional functions, the institutional process, as well as ceremonial situations; nonformal language is one in which we express varying degrees of subjectivity and intimacy, with a freer expression in terms of words, phrases, structures, and even subjects.

What is the appropriate language for the situation? This is an important decision that requires social sensitivity.[5] Good common sense advice is to use formal language in work and institutional situations and use nonformal language when in intimate groups and relaxed social settings. Young people in the process of integrating into work often cannot abandon nonformal language or decide when it is appropriate in the organizational environment. It is better for them to learn as quickly as possible because that is how they become professionals.

Use formal language:

- In professional environments, especially in crises or when dealing with important or delicate matters. In other words, when the subject is "serious." It is important to acquire the sensitivity to perceive seriousness.
- In important negotiations, especially when the participants are not intimate.
- When in doubt about the level of formality required. In this case, start with formal language and only move to informal language if the situation clearly shows that it is acceptable.

Use nonformal language whenever possible, because informality creates a more pleasant and productive environment. For example, a person in a doctor's office usually feels stressed and vulnerable. If the doctor adopts formal language, this may increase the patient's discomfort. At the same time, the consultation creates an intimate relationship. Therefore, informal and respectful language is most appropriate in the doctor-patient conversation.

Denotation versus connotation. "Let's have a glass of champagne." This phrase has a denotative meaning, which is the objective, direct, and neutral meaning that each word has in the dictionary. But, inevitably, like any other phrase or word, it has a connotative meaning—a symbolic or extended one that goes beyond words. Connotative meaning derives from emotional or cultural associations.

The correct manipulation of connotation gives color to words and phrases, appeals to fantasy and imagination and amplifies the effect of the message. The exercise below will give you an idea of how to use connotation to benefit your messages.

Word choices and social sensitivity. Thanks to democracy and social development, many (not all) people who suffered discrimination before are now treated with the respect they deserve. In place of the offensive language that was used to refer to people, today there are "vocabulary requirements," that is, a better understanding of inclusive language and recognition of the harm that words can cause, especially to minorities. We now have the vocabulary to correctly refer to others, including indications of gender, ethnicity, sexual orientation, physical characteristics, social origin, etc.[6]

Language is constantly evolving to provide the most appropriate responses to new social demands and expectations. The person who is genuinely concerned about living happily and productively in the groups they participate in adjusts to new ways of expressing themselves.

Does your choice of words and social sensitivity show people that you respect them, or perhaps invite people to see you as a "safe space" for conversation? To achieve excellence in communication, learn and familiarize yourself with these new words, new ways of treating people, and new attitudes for living in society.

Nonverbal Communications

Nonverbal communication regulates social interactions through cues that indicate emotions, social hierarchy, dominance or status, and levels of openness or proximity to dialogue. It necessarily complements verbal communication and is the most effective way of demonstrating acceptance, love, affection, approval, or the opposite of all of these.[2]

Some nonverbal expressions are under a person's control; others are involuntary behaviors, often unconscious and automatic. The rate of control of nonverbal expression depends on individual ability. Experienced actors and actresses can control their emotional state and present feelings opposite to what they are feeling. At the same time, they can pretend to be a person with emotions they will never feel and who will seem like real people to us.

If you want to improve your conversation skills:

1) Become aware of the general positive nonverbal cues.

Ask yourself: what are the nonverbal signals from people that make me feel good?

2) Become aware of the main nonverbal signals that you usually send;

3) Start sending positive signals and persist until you incorporate the habit is completely;

4) Learn to manipulate all elements of nonverbal communication properly. Use the list below.

What are the elements of nonverbal communication? Here's a partial list:[2]

- Facial expressions
- Gestures
- Body posture
- Clothing and appearance
- Accessories (jewelry, watches, or glasses)
- Personal proximity in space
- Touch
- Eye contact
- Vocal modulation and dynamics
- Silence

Remember how the doctor received the mother and daughter? He didn't look at them—a disrespectful and offensive nonverbal signal. Thus, it did not help improve the communication during that time.

Some useful tips on nonverbal communication:

- Back straight, shoulders back, head up. This is the attitude of someone who respects themselves and earns the respect of others.[7]
- Show bodily signs of receptivity and openness. It means disarming facial expressions, friendly eye contact, and peaceful, cooperative gestures.
- Learn to act. You will have to adapt your nonverbal communication to different situations, so being a social actor is an aptitude requirement.
- Modulation in voice volume and dynamics, that is, the flow and speed of words, can indicate hesitation, insecurity, aggressiveness, arrogance— or the opposite of all of these. Try to train your speech to express yourself with adequate volume so that people hear you but don't feel bothered by a high volume. Also try to vary the volume so as not to have a monotonous and boring voice. Maintain an appropriate pace and, above all, avoid the voices that we all know well: the intonation of arrogance, aggressiveness, irony and disregard of other people.

You can include the environment and objects in the list. Suppose you are an entrepreneur and will receive a potential client for the company. You are starting a negotiation for a service and know the client's main quality requirements are order and control of the service. Before the client arrives, you can set up the environment of your office to present it as orderly and professional.

As an addition to keep your office clean and well-kept, you can post photos of your staff on duty at other organizations, showing discipline, cleanliness, and order. Through these visual elements, you will communicate the idea without words, that is, in the best way: visually, with a strong appeal to non rational perception.

You can also use objects to communicate. In the case of the customer's visit, display objects in your office that represent you as a committed, efficient, and customer-oriented person. Just put your creativity to work, and you will find objects to reinforce your ideas and messages.

Rapport

Relationships are much more important than communication, which is the simple exchange of messages. But it means nothing or everything, depending on the relationship. For example, why might some people touch your hair, kiss your face, say nasty things, criticize, and scold you? It depends on rapport, which can be defined as a state of mutual trust, respect, and understanding between individuals, which promotes a climate where communication flows smoothly, ideas are exchanged openly, and both parties feel comfortable and engaged.[8]

Rapport is the core of a relationship and results from a history of interactions. The objective of seeking excellence in personal communication is to achieve rapport and create solid relationships for life.

The benefits of rapport include:

- *Greater effectiveness in communication.* All parties' reasons and personal situations are easily understood, errors are corrected without harm, feedback is faster and clearer, etc.
- *Promotion of intimacy, emotional support, and a sense of belonging.* This impacts personal well-being, self-image, self-confidence, etc.
- *Building the basis for professional and social partnerships.* That will increase the opportunities offered to people and promote their potential for improvement.

In short, a good relationship is the most important factor for career success. Research by Pamela Laird has shown that factors such as hard work, talent, and education, although important, play a less significant role in achieving success than people previously believed. Social networks make a difference and provide access to opportunities, information, and resources.[9]

Here is a short, true story for your consideration: As an associate consultant at the HR company, I informed myself about clients' executive recruitment processes. The curricula vitae (CVs) arrived to be offered to clients, who screened them and called candidates for interviews. The recruiter complained that a specific CV was regularly offered but never resulted in a single interview. I looked at the résumé and immediately saw that the person was highly qualified academically and professionally.

I asked the recruiter, "Why is this candidate not called for interviews?"

She replied that "the market had restrictions against the professional."

I commented, "How does this happen? The HR market represents more than one hundred thousand people in the city! Is it possible for the candidate to be known by all these people?"

"He is not known personally," she said, "But people know his reputation, which probably has negative implications."

This shows that communication spreads through social networks, and even strangers often have something to say about us. What they say will depend on what we do and what we communicate. For example, suppose the doctor had not redeemed himself in segment three. What would have happened? Certainly, the mother and daughter would have formed a bad image of him. We can imagine a chain like this:

Step 1: Person A (the mother) talks to Person B (a friend) and tells her about the incident and the doctor's inappropriate behavior.

Step 2: Person C, a colleague of Person B, is looking for a doctor to consult with and considers our doctor. Person B refers to what happened to Person A.

Step 3: Person C selects another doctor from the same clinic, goes with her son to a consultation, and receives caring attention. So, she tells Person D there are two pediatricians in that clinic, one whom she recommends and another whom she does not.

Thus, the person on the third level of the chain of connections will influence the doctor's attractiveness to clients. Social media research shows that we are affected positively or negatively by two different groups of people: the strong-ties group and the weak-ties group. While those with strong ties (close friends and family) provide support, those with weak ties often connect us to new information and opportunities.[10,11]

We can extract a key piece of advice from the research: *Networking makes a real difference in your career and life. Invest in creating good rapport in any opportunity that social life offers.*

Empathy And Openness

Empathy is the ability to identify and experience others' sentiments, a component of our human neural structure. By identifying ourselves with others, through behavior, verbal, and nonverbal cues, empathy develops naturally, by mirroring their happiness, pain, sadness, fear, etc.

Observing a painful grimace may activate neurons in our own brain and we may experience what the other is feeling. This natural behavior will be absent in people with abnormal brain structures.[12]

Self-awareness and self-reflection fuel empathy because comprehending our sentiments permits us to identify similarities in other people. That's why the millennium wisdom proverb says that "to know thyself is to know all men."

Empathy is a requirement for excellence in communication and the creation of real rapport. If a person is seriously committed to improving their conversation skills, they will have to face the challenge of increasing their empathy. In chapter 5 the concept and good practices of empathy will be discussed in more details.

Empathy goes hand in hand with openness, which is self-disclosure, "the voluntary communication of personal information about oneself," and the willingness to accept expression from others.[13]

Openness includes:

- Honesty and transparency: sharing information and feelings sincerely.
- Self-disclosure: revealing personal thoughts and experiences.
- Active listening: paying close attention, and understanding the other person's perspective.
- Open communication: promoting trust, intimacy, and stronger relationships.

Remember the doctor's apology: "Sorry, Ma'am. I have to apologize. I didn't know she couldn't hear or speak. I'm quite stressed due to a medical incident I was involved in an hour ago. That's why I acted rudely." It makes a real difference. He was transparent in stating that he was stressed; he opened up, acknowledging that he was rude.

Active Listening

Active listening is much more than listening, which is an automatic process leading to automatic responses in everyday situations,[14] such as: "Where's the book?" "Here it is."Active listening goes far beyond that, as the dialogue below between Mary and Ethan demonstrates. They are scheduled to make a presentation for the company and the dialogue that comes before that did not bring much benefit to Mary, as we will see:

Mary: I'm a very shy person.

Ethan: Me too, but not much. Don't worry; we'll do well in front of the group.

In the dialogue, Ethan listened but didn't realize how shy Mary was. In fact, it will be a very stressful challenge for the first person to be in front of the group, and they didn't sleep a minute last night.

The person who wants to improve their communication skills has to acquire the sensitivity to perceive when to just hear, when to listen, and when to listen actively, which means to listen deeply and truthfully. Active listening is an essential component of openness, empathy, and the construction of rapport. There will never be real communication if active listening is not part of the process.[15] In Chapter 5, the theme will be discussed in more detail.

Chapter Summary

- The selection of correct content, phrases, and words plays an important role in the communication process, but it is only one aspect.
- To achieve excellence in conversation, it is necessary to adopt a complete communication model. This involves attitudes, verbal and nonverbal messages, and even manipulating objects and the environment to communicate.
- Verbal communication requires sensitivity to select the right content, understand the connotative dimension of words, and develop vocabulary suitable for different situations and people.
- Nonverbal communication necessarily complements words and sentences and includes facial expression, gestures, body posture, voice modulation, and even silence.
- Communication and relationships influence each other, creating virtual or vicious cycles that will affect personal performance at work and in life. This means that the relationship you have with a person makes communication easier or more difficult; and communication itself improves or hinders the relationship. The worse the relationship, the more difficult the

communication and the more difficult it is, the more difficult it is to establish a good relationship. It's the vicious cycle. The opposite is the virtuous cycle where each sphere contributes to the efficiency of the other.

- Remember that relationships are more important than communication; focusing on creating rapport at every social opportunity is wise behavior practiced by winners.

- Being open, empathetic, and engaged in active listening is a requirement to create rapport and open the social doors to productive participation and leadership.

Action Steps

Understanding "Different People"

Many times we ask ourselves, why are they this way? And we do not have the faintest idea about people's choices of clothing, styles, behaviors, ideas, and so on. Let's do an exercise that will help you improve your understanding of strangers.

Step 1: Select two people from your work or social group that you have not particularly bonded with. Focus on the people whose "differences" keep you apart.

Step 2: Prepare conversation starters. Then, create ample opportunities and approach each one of those people.

Step 3: With no hurry, engage these people in conversation and express curiosity about the characteristics that make the person "different" and ask friendly questions about them.

Your Rate Of Openness

What is your rate of openness? This is a question that would be best answered by others, right? Your openness rate is based on the objective and subjective signs you express through your discourse, body language, actions, even history and social position.

Step 1: Choose three to five colleagues whose opinions you consider relevant.

Step 2: Speak to each one in a disarming way and ask them to evaluate your rate of openness on a 1–5 scale, considering:

- Verbal messages
- Nonverbal messages
- General look
- Actions
- Other

Step 3: Discuss the evaluation with each one, trying to just listen and ask meaningful questions.

3

AN EXTROVERT'S CONVERSATION FLOW

HOW TO INITIATE, MAINTAIN, AND CONCLUDE A THRIVING CONVERSATION

When I was 18, I correctly imagined that a person who acquires competence in sales increases their potential for career success in any area. So, I decided to dedicate myself to sales for a while. I soon found a job, received the training and sales kit, and started working, or better said, I started trying to work.

The task was simple: the firm had a registry of families with children in their final years of primary school, about to enter secondary school. I had to knock on the door to be able to talk to the children's parents. If I passed the first contact test, I had to chat with the parent and offer enrollment in a student incentive club that provided books, private lessons, and similar benefits.

My problem was that I was shy, and I only remembered that when I arrived at the house with my briefcase and sales kit. I thought about a thousand things before knocking on the door:

- I'll get in the way.
- People must be eating, sleeping, bathing, and watching TV.
- They'll think I'm inappropriate, a clueless person.
- People are going to be mad at my offer because money is hard to come by these days.
- Will they think it's a scam?
- Maybe they don't like the way I look.

As the courage didn't come, all I could do was leave this house, where contact was difficult, and go to another, where things might be easier. With each house I passed on, I lost my sales commission.

If I had someone to help me, maybe things would have been easier: a father or mother to hold my hand and go with me to knock on the door; an experienced boss who could give me caring encouragement; perhaps a more experienced salesperson to do the sales with me. How difficult life is for those who don't have social support!

A few days later, I ran into an old sales colleague who could go door-to-door, talk to people, and sell that incentive plan. I told him I couldn't sell it because I was a little shy. "Are you shy, man?" he said. "Bad for you. Get rid of it." I replied that it was not that easy. "Do you want to be extroverted?" He continued. "Act like an extrovert; no one will do it for you."

I only realized the tremendous validity of this intuitive advice twenty years later, reading Aristotle.[1] He posited that our qualities come from what we do; that is, by doing the right things, you can transform your thoughts, feelings, and behaviors.

"... for from the things we do we acquire the qualities corresponding to them, e.g., by building houses we become builders, and by playing the lute, we become lute-players; so too by doing just acts we become just, and by doing temperate acts, temperate..." (Nicomachean Ethics, Book II, 1.1103a25-30)[1]

Behavioral researchers confirm that although shyness is innate in 20% of babies, this characteristic can be transformed by correct behavior; shy babies can be bold adults; "temperament is not destiny."[2]

As time passed and I was pressured by necessity, I progressively acted like an extroverted person at work, took some courses, and ended up learning to overcome fear. Today, I would say that, if necessary, I could even contact the president to sell underwear.

Cycle Of Thriving Conversation

On 1% of occasions, fear is a great friend, but on 99% of occasions, it is a great enemy that paralyzes us, preventing us from achieving good things at work and in our social lives. It prevented me from approaching those people, starting productive and rewarding conversations, and achieving my sales goals. By breaking this barrier, the person not only initiates relationships more easily and naturally but also remains more relaxed and happy during the interactive process.

If you don't take the initiative to approach people, the conversation may not happen. So, having the courage to get closer is necessary, but it is not enough. It's the starting point, but we need to acquire the skills to efficiently take the conversation to the end.

As Schegloff notes, conversation happens in a flow that is not random, as it contains recognizable patterns. This process includes a rich repertoire of cues, such as intonation and facial expressions, that help people manage their behavior and solve problems to ensure a smooth and successful conversation.[3]

Let's consider the conversation as a sequence of three parts: initiation, development, and closure. In each of them we can adopt some natural and already identified behaviors so that the final result is satisfactory and brings gratification to both parties.

We will discuss some tips that may be useful in each part, but with two very important initial pieces of advice:

- Don't try to be smart, funny, witty, and magnetic. Choose spontaneity and simplicity.
- Do not apply techniques in a simplistic way. For example, if you use praise as a technique, it will quickly be unmasked and negatively affect your image, showing you as a manipulative person.

Starting Like An Extrovert

I took a course on humor improvisation techniques, which taught me one important thing: When entering the stage to interact with your scene partners, start without fuss. Instead of trying to approach someone in a memorable way, try to approach them in a discreet way, so that they are willing to talk and feel comfortable with it.

The benefits of such an approach are:

- It avoids problems in the first encounter, such as activating the person's fear and alert system.
- The interlocutor does not develop any expectations of you and progresively values your presence in the conversation, as you listen and speak with empathy and care.
- It accelerates the process of creating rapport.

Just Start Naturally

There are some natural rules for starting conversations the right way. You can find good practical advice on the subject on the web from different sources.[4,5] It's always good to read these practical tips for ideas, but there are some common fundamentals. Let's discuss them.

Evaluate The Situation

It is important to only begin a conversation when the situation calls for it naturally. Pay attention to time and place, and observe the person with whom you plan to engage. Make sure to respect their privacy and do not bother them if they seem to be occupied. If you are at a conference where networking is encouraged, it is expected that you engage with other attendees. But if someone is quietly reading a book in a park, perhaps you should let them be.

Respect other people's privacy and situations. For example, do not bother occupied people with momentous, inopportune conversation. Also, do not try to engage someone in chit-chat if they seem worried about something. Pay attention to the nonverbal signs of potential interlocutors.

Observe People And Find Opportunities To Interact With Them

By paying attention to people, you can identify good opportunities to start a worthwhile conversation. For example, you observe similarities between you and the person, and you can refer to this, which will surely attract the interlocutor's attention. Or you can notice something the person did or said that deserves praise—and you can start the conversation with praise, something that all people like.

Suppose you also notice something the person did or said that deserves thanks. Thanking the person for something is also a great start because every human being is gratified by a sincere thank you. Finally, you might notice something the person said that interests you. Mentioning this interest to the person adds value to what they said.

Don't Forget To Listen Actively

Remember that active listening is one of the pillars of good communication. At the beginning of the conversation, it already plays a very important role, because people who know how to listen gain sympathy more easily and avoid mistakes caused by a lack of knowledge about the interlocutor. If you have no idea about the interlocutor's feelings, values and ideas, you run a greater risk of saying the wrong things, which will cause discomfort in the initial phase.

Be Receptive And Present The Appropriate Emotion

Start the conversation from the inside out: control your emotions and attitude to show a receptive, friendly, and open face. Always set your face with the appropriate expression (smiling, sympathy, intrigue, etc.) for the situation: a sad and discreet smile for a funeral, an expectant smile in a new group, a happy smile in a tour group, and a neutral smile in the transient group in the elevator.

Start With The Basics

Take the initiative, with the appropriate greeting. It can be a simple "Hi," "Hello," or "How is it going?"

Be Prepared The Right Way

Be prepared to continue the dialogue. It basically means having a few topics ready that fit the situation. Examples of continuing after saying hello:

In a club:

- This DJ has great beats. Do you like this type of music?
- You are drinking my favorite drink.
- Are you celebrating any occasions today?

In a seminar, among strangers:

- Let me sit in front. I have high expectations for this seminar.
- Are you connected with any companies in the sector? (of solar energy, the object of the seminar).
- Have you ever attended a seminar by Dr. XYZ?

At a funeral:

- I am very sad. I worked with him for twenty years.
- How did you know so-and-so?

There is an important point: These are just examples, never formulas. Do not use formulas, for they kill your spontaneity. In *The Godfather* movie, there is a scene in which the character Luca Brasi (Lenny Montana) appears anxiously rehearsing a speech to congratulate Don

Corleone on his daughter's wedding. It is funny, because people quickly realized that the speech was rehearsed, but it didn't come out according to what was memorized. It became robotic and unnatural speech.[6]

So, do not rehearse based on formulas or texts. Get the idea and do it your way spontaneously; do not be afraid of making errors. The most important thing is the right attitude and a firm desire to share experiences and emotions with other people.

Ask The Right Questions

Use the right questions to engage people in conversation. Questions are one of the best ways of establishing connections, but they require social sensibility. For example:

Starting a conversation with a classmate at a seminar:

- Wrong

"Did you graduate in this field?" The person can feel challenged in his competency.

- Right

"Can you help me if I don't understand anything? I am new in the field." Asking for help is always good because it awakens the scout in each of us. Human beings are naturally supportive. Unsupportive people are the exception.

So, make sure that the question is appropriate, that it will not embarrass the person, that it will not be invasive, and that it will not disturb the person. Evaluate the situation before asking questions. For example, asking "What time is it?" may be inappropriate if the person is carrying a heavy object or offensive if they just arrived slightly late for the meeting. Anyway, ask questions, but keep your social sensitivity alert.

Manifest After Other's Expressions Or Actions

Be alert and attentive to other people's nonverbal or verbal expressions, and react positively.

Here are some examples:

- A young woman shows clear nonverbal signs of discomfort and stress. You can approach her and ask if everything is okay and whether you can help in any way.
- A man asks a pertinent question in a seminar: You can approach him and tell him you appreciate the question because it presents ideas you have not thought about yet.
- A person proffers an opinion in a social meeting. You can approach them and tell them you agree with their opinion.

Conversation Development: Conquer Interlocutors' Attention And Interest

The conversation must maintain an adequate flow so that it does not end before the right moment or continue beyond that. Always keep in mind the question: Why are we engaging in this conversation? A clear perception of the purpose of the meeting will dictate the appropriate flow and duration. In my vision, there are two main enemies of conversation that must be vigorously fought for it to fully achieve its purpose: toxicity, inattention, and boredom.

<u>Toxicity</u>

Toxicity is the presence of unpleasant, exhausting emotions among participants. Inappropriate topics, the wrong choice of words, or the expression of disturbing ideas can give rise to these emotions. Remember that the conversation should flow pleasantly, even in conflicting or sad situations—for example, hope in a conflict resolution conversation or a conversation about a sad topic.

The rule is: don't let toxic emotions surface; keep pleasant emotions prominent. For example, a boss who is firing an employee might say, "I'm really upset that I had to do this because I really like you and appreciate our time together."

What should we do when a toxic emotion appears? Here are three suggestions:

- Change the subject in a courteous manner.
- Reinterpret the other person's speech to give it a positive tone.
- Kindly ask your interlocutors for help in maintaining the atmosphere. Remind them of the conversation's purpose and the relationship's importance.

Remember that judgments and blame are some of the major causes of toxicity and negativity in communication.[7] Avoid expressing them, and help your interlocutors do so as well.

<u>Boredom</u>

If the interlocutor, for any reason, loses attention, the conversation tends to decrease in quality. Be alert to the nonverbal and verbal signals of inattention. Is the interlocutor bothered? Are they worried about any toxic emotions? Do they feel that the conversation is not worth it? There are some very simple but effective ways to make the interlocutors return to the conversation, such as, for example, sharing your vulnerabilities.[8]

As soon as you notice signs of inattention, look for a way to solve the problem. Examples of signs of inattention are looking at the clock, looking at the cell phone, talking to colleagues, looking down, physical restlessness, and yawning. Here are some suggestions on how to react appropriately:

- Politely ask the interlocutor if you are boring them or if the subject is not interesting.
- Ask the person if they would prefer to talk another day.
- Make an open question about the subject.
- Say something that surprises the interlocutor, for example, a shocking affirmation or a personal revelation.

For example, the therapist noticed that my friend lost contact with him, caught up in his repetitive talk of complaining and victimization. Then he excused himself and told him, "Your problems aren't going to be solved; you're out of luck." Surprised, my friend stopped ruminating and looked at the therapist, actually willing to listen to him.

- Tell a short anecdote about something funny that happened to you that is related to the topic you are talking about.

Suppose you are talking to people about stressful situations, and you say: "Did you know that I was once attacked by a clown on the street? Very stressful." There is a high probability that people will pay attention.

- *Use sound contrast*: mute, increase or decrease the volume of your voice, increase or decrease the speed of your speech flow. Every time you introduce changes, like sound vs. silence,

increasing voice volume or speed, people
wake up.

Jonathan Swift (1667–1745) offers humorous and satirical
commentary on the superficiality of upper-class
conversation in early 18th-century England. Although it
was not intended to show how to get rid of boredom in
conversation, several of his comments remain surprisingly
relevant.[9] Here are some of them:

Avoid excessive self-importance. Talking exaggeratedly about
yourself, your achievements, activities, and possessions
makes your speech uninteresting.

Beware of jargon and obscure references. This is using
conversation to impress other people. Avoid technical
references or subjects, except when between peers, in
appropriate places (e.g., a conference).

Don't monopolize the conversation. Trying to dominate
conversations by ignoring others' attempts to speak is the
best way to bore people. Remember the importance of
actively listening and allowing others to contribute.

Beware of emotional extremes. Swift's characters often express
exaggerated emotions, from excessive flattery to feigned
outrage. This suggests that a balanced and genuine
emotional tone can keep the conversation engaging.

Embrace intellectual curiosity. Swift's characters often lack
genuine curiosity about the world or the people they
converse with. Genuine curiosity leads to good questions

and real active listening. Remember, nobody gets bored when talking about himself.

One of the secrets to avoiding boredom is variety.

- Vary the subjects.
- Change the volume and rhythm of your voice.
- Alter your attitudes; for example, being a chronically critical or complaining person is a huge bummer.
- Vary your mood, such as by avoiding being serious or funny all the time.

Closure: What Is Next

When the purpose of the conversation is fulfilled, it is time to end. Whether it's a job interview, a business meeting, a meeting with the school principal, or a celebratory family lunch, there is a right time to finish. When is it? There is no rule but to apply your feelings and social sensitivity. If the meeting lasts longer than needed, it will not have a happy ending. Be cautious.

Before ending the meeting, it is important to resolve any bad feelings or misunderstandings that arose during it. For example, at some point in the conversation, you expressed an opinion about separate schools for immigrant children in their first years in the country. You realized that your idea on the subject was not fully understood, but the conversation took a different direction, and you did not have the opportunity to clarify your point of view.

You feel that some people may have a wrong idea about you, thinking you are a prejudiced person. So, take the chance now, at the closure, to clarify your position with those people. Conversations must end in a positive emotional climate, which means people must want to repeat the experience. Let good emotions abound, say the right words (e.g., "Thanks, it was a nice day, I learned a lot," or "I had a lot of fun"), and end it.

Chapter Summary

This chapter explores how to initiate, maintain, and conclude successful conversations. Here are the key takeaways:

- *Overcoming shyness:* Don't let shyness hold you back. Act extroverted to learn to be extroverted and to build confidence and social skills.
- *Starting on the right foot:* First impressions matter, but they are not definitive, since you can (and must) fix communication errors. Be friendly and respectful, and adapt your approach to the situation.
- *Natural conversation flow:* Conversations progress in stages. Use tips and questions to keep things flowing smoothly. Prioritize spontaneity and authenticity over trying to "shine."

Maintaining Engagement:

- *Avoid toxicity:* Steer clear of negativity and unpleasant emotions. Focus on positive and productive communication. Use nonverbal cues like smiles to project a positive attitude.
- *Combat inattention:* Watch for signs of disinterest and use techniques like open questions or personal anecdotes to reengage your audience.
- *Banish boredom:* Avoid topics and behaviors that bore others. Embrace intellectual curiosity and keep things varied.
- *Conclusion:* End conversations at the right time, on a high. Resolve any misunderstandings and leave a positive impression.

Additional Tips:

- Compliment genuinely, not just to win people over.
- Ask thoughtful questions to spark conversation and build rapport.

Action Steps

Act Like An Extrovert

Why are some people extroverts? They are extroverts because they act as extroverts. Qualities, although they can have an innate dimension, are mostly the result of action. And actions are manageable. So, you can manage your actions to reach the desirable qualities.

Steps

1. Take one situation where you frequently participate and would like to act like an extrovert.
2. Identify one thing an extrovert usually does in this situation.
3. Do this action the next time you are in this situation. Repeat the exercise, adding other things an extrovert does in the situation.

Using Your Experience

Many times, people underestimate and underuse their own experience. Certainly, anyone may have interesting things to say about many subjects. Let's check out the steps to do it:

1. Think about three true, interesting stories that happened to you.
2. Identify the subjects to which these stories are related.
3. In the first opportunity the subject arises, tell one story.
4. Repeat the experience.

4

ASSERT YOURSELF!

HOW TO USE YOUR VOICE TO GET RESPECT FROM OTHERS

My friend was a teacher at an elementary school on the outskirts of a big city. She truly cared about her students and wanted them to grow. She began to have problems with a teenager who was not only inattentive and uninterested in lessons and exercises but also disruptive in class. So, she made a first attempt to talk seriously with the boy, but to no avail. She realized that solving the problem was beyond her possibilities and resources and mentioned to a colleague that she was considering calling the student's parents for a conversation.

"You're going crazy," said the colleague. "Don't you know who his parents are? They are a very scandalous couple, who complain about everything and treat you as if you were their employee, in addition to threatening to sue the school for anything. You are going to summon them to come to the school to resolve their son's problem?!"

"Why not? This is my responsibility, and no one can criticize me for doing my job," said my friend, who sent a request to the boy's parents' house, asking them to come to school. To everyone's surprise, two days later, the parents were there, dressed appropriately and with expressions of interest. The teacher had a good conversation with them, noticed they were really interested in their son's education, and soon after began to observe a change in the student's behavior.

This is the type of teacher that makes a difference in our lives.

- She did not remain passive in the face of something wrong.
- She demonstrated self-respect, acceptance of her social role, and her natural right, as a citizen, to do what is correct.
- She also showed the courage to act despite the boy's father's fame.
- She showed respect for the boy's parents. (Is there anything more disrespectful than letting their child fail in education?)
- Tell me what you think about the two questions below:
- Do you think the teacher earned the respect of the boy's relatives?
- And how about the respect of others in the school's structure?

The teacher gained respect and voice on merit because she was *assertive*. This is the quality of the person who acts affirmatively, with *assertiveness*, that can be defined as "the ability to express your needs, wants, and feelings directly, honestly, and confidently, while respecting the rights of others".[1]

It is the opposite of passivity and aggressiveness, and so it is the only correct way to communicate if you want to build valuable relationships for life. If you are passive, others will not respect you, even if they love you. If you are aggressive, you will make enemies along your life's journey, and this will certainly bring you all kinds of problems. But if you are an assertive person, you will make your voice heard peacefully and create the best relationships possible in the situation. So, if you want to be a good communicator, you need to develop assertiveness.

The benefits of assertiveness have been well documented by researchers, such as:

- Increased self-esteem and confidence: assertively expressing yourself can lead to a feeling of accomplishment and self-worth.[1]
- Improved communication and relationships: When you communicate assertively, you're more likely to be understood and have your needs met, fostering stronger relationships.[2]
- Reduced stress and anxiety: Assertiveness allows

you to effectively manage difficult situations, leading to lower stress and anxiety levels.[3]

- Greater ability to set boundaries: By assertively communicating your limits, you can protect yourself from being taken advantage of.[3]
- Increased personal effectiveness: Assertiveness helps you achieve your goals by enabling you to advocate for yourself and negotiate effectively.[1]

In summary, assertive communication will make your messages more transparent and clearer; others will better know what you think, want or don't want, and value. At the same time, your personal power will increase, giving you a voice and place in life events and having your legitimate choices respected and fulfilled. You will say no when appropriate, and yes when you want and can.

Can you imagine the importance of this in your daily life?

Aggressive, Passive, And Assertive Behavior

The only rational and emotionally mature behavioral choice is to be assertive, with which you will earn the respect you deserve and, in most cases, the sympathy and admiration of others.

What are the main differences between these three types of behavior?

Aggressive Behavior

- Harshness with words, tone of voice, and messages.
- Disregarding other people's voices, ideas, and presence.
- Trying to get the word out before others and monopolize the conversation.
- Giving unsolicited and unwanted suggestions, advice, criticism, and opinions.
- Confronting others clearly and inappropriately.
- Using derogatory nicknames, treatments, or aggressive verbal expressions such as irony, sarcasm, and imitations.
- Making offensive jokes.
- Being authoritarian, imposing unnecessary and non-rational rules.

Passive Behavior

- Staying silent when you should speak.
- Giving involuntarily.
- Making chronic efforts to please others.
- Avoiding necessary and appropriate criticism, advice, and opinions.
- Avoiding confrontation, even when necessary and rational.
- Accepting bullying and cheating.
- Giving up your rights and prerogatives involuntarily.

Assertive Behavior

- Take the floor whenever necessary and always with kindness and diplomacy.
- Defend your rights and prerogatives.
- Consider and pay attention to the rights and prerogatives of others.
- Strive to please others as long as their demands are legitimate, and this does not imply giving up your space or prerogatives.

Assertive behavior is the only choice to be present in life, respected by yourself and others. You will avoid doing what you did not choose and will live in a more pleasant and productive way.

Assertiveness In Social Life

Lucy loves her friend Mary but is not very comfortable with one aspect of her behavior. Mary is very bossy, and there is only one way to maintain a peaceful relationship with her: by doing what she wants.

In the past, until the end of adolescence, the friendship was nurtured with constant contact, without any major problems, as Mary is an interesting person and always had good ideas about what to do. But, over time and with the beginning of her career as a lawyer after college, Lucy changed and no longer likes to accept things passively, especially because she has a wide range of interests.

Thus, Lucy avoids contact with Mary a little but misses her genuine friendship with someone outside the sphere of law. Mary also misses her friend's company, but realizes that Lucy avoids her and is embarrassed to insist on the invitations.

Tell me, reader, what to do?

To me, it seems that there are two people with inappropriate behavior here: Mary, who is too aggressive in pursuing her interests, and Lucy, who is too passive in social life, despite being a leader with adequate skills at work.

There is no other way to resolve the problem than by taking the initiative to engage in dialogue. There's a good chance the conversation won't be very pleasant, but it will clarify things.

Lucy has to say yes; she has been avoiding her friend and misses her company. She should be clear and specific about her reasons for avoidance and what she wants from the relationship. Mary should listen carefully, admit her guilt, and explain her reason, if any; she must also tell her friend what she wants and what she commits to doing.

If they both really value the relationship and want to improve it, dialogue will bring good results.

Assertiveness At Work

Bill and Ted are interns in the logistics department of a large multinational company. Both are well qualified, engaged in work, responsible, and intelligent. Their boss, John, will have to select one of them for a recently opened position in a distant unit. This will be a real step towards career advancement for the chosen one. But it won't be easy for those chosen to overcome the challenge, mainly because in that unit people work under pressure and stress is high.

John has been analyzing Bill and Ted's behavioral profiles. Ted is much more relaxed, more present in the boss's office, and more easily accepts his ideas and decisions. But John often feels like Ted doesn't say exactly what he's feeling or thinking and keeps silent to please the boss. In turn, Bill is not always easy to deal with; he has more difficulty accepting some of his boss's instructions, requires a little more effort to be convinced, and is not very present in his boss's office. At the same time, he says what he thinks and feels, even if they are not pleasant words for the boss.

Boss's decision: Bill was chosen. "Well, I admire them both and respect them for their competence," said John. "Bill is not easy to communicate with, but I think he is the right choice for that busy unit. His way of telling things clearly and firmly influenced my decision. I was afraid that Ted wouldn't be able to control some of the rude but kind people we have in the unit." In other words, John chose the most assertive guy. John thinks that Bill would not only be able to control rude people, but also assert needs and desires. Bill would likely be able to clearly set limits and deadlines and maintain respect for himself and others in addition to earning their respect.

Requirements For Assertive Behavior

Acting and communicating assertively requires two main qualities: courage and respect, and these focus on you and others, as in the illustration.

Courage	Respect
• To accept your own desires, impulses, needs, values, and beliefs. • To express to others, and eventually to confront them.	• For yourself • For others

Courage To Accept Yourself

Some people cannot be assertive because they live with internal conflicts, denying their desires, impulses, needs, values, and beliefs. For example, a person lacks self-confidence because they belong to a discriminated minority. Instead of facing a problematic situation, this person may not be fully prepared to assertively ask others to avoid disrespectful actions against their minority group.

Internal conflicts occur mainly when education or group pressures impose ideas or feelings that one does not naturally assimilate. Self-denying can manifest as stress in many ways, from neglecting basic physical needs like sleep or healthy eating to suppressing emotions or personal goals. It can result in health problems[4] and can also erode a person's sense of self-esteem, making it difficult to stand up for oneself and be assertive with others.[5]

In the case of self-denying, the person has nothing to want from others, nothing to demand, and nothing to impose. They simply do not seek anything for themselves and accept the impositions that come from outside—or run away from them without confrontation. Socrates' statement that man is his greatest enemy applies perfectly.[6]

Courage To Express And Confront Others

Assertiveness also requires courage to reveal your inner intentions to others. This can be worrying because every other person has boundaries to protect, many have power, and many can be aggressive to varying degrees.

Furthermore, we all care about the love and approval of others, and some are afraid that revealing our desires, needs, values, and preferences may lead others to stop giving them to us. Imagine how hard it is to say no to your parents, siblings, dear friends, bosses, and colleagues! This natural difficulty, combined with a weak ability to assert oneself, makes many people victims of exploitative mothers, wives, husbands, bosses, and friends.

Ultimately, this inability to speak and act assertively works against the exploiters who bully the non-assertive person. For example:

a) The authoritarian boss is surprised by mistakes that could oust him from his position; the non-assertive person didn't have the courage to contradict him and this led to these mistakes;

b) Intimidating parents can be abandoned by children who have lost love for them because they have suffered oppression;

c) Blackmailers can be ambushed by people who did not have the courage to confront them directly, and accumulated hurt and anger;

d) Friends turn into enemies when one harbors resentment for not having their needs accommodated simply because they were not able to communicate with them at all.

Here are two tips for developing an emotional foundation for assertiveness:

- Make the necessary effort to identify and understand what you deny about yourself.
- Develop the courage to say what you want to others and confront them when necessary.

Consider that our fears may be primarily the result of Automatic Negative Thoughts (ANTs), as postulated by Aaron T. Beck, a pioneer in cognitive behavioral therapy (CBT). ANTs are negative and distorted thoughts that automatically pop into our heads, often leading to emotional suffering. These thoughts are negative self-talk that distort reality.[7]

Self-Respect

Self-respect can be defined as an individual's positive regard for themselves and their inherent worth. It involves believing that you deserve to be treated with respect and having the confidence to stand up for your needs and boundaries.[8] It is one of the foundations of assertive action and communication.

Here are some behaviors that are characteristic of self-respect:

- Adopting self-respectful language. It includes not devaluing yourself or diminishing your qualities and potential.
- Being careful with opinions and comments to preserve an image of competence and professionalism.
- Maintaining consistency between your speech and actions.
- Responding appropriately, with courtesy and diplomacy, to any unfair criticism, negative opinion of yourself, or misinterpretation of your words or actions.

Respect For Others

Respect for others complements the basic requirements

for assertive behavior. It is the first rule to be observed in any situation.

Respect for others includes:

- Listening to them carefully and considering their messages effectively.
- Maintaining awareness of others' emotional situations to appropriately approach communication with them.
- Adopting appropriate tone and style in speech.
- Respecting the boundaries, privacy, and expressed wishes and interests of others.
- Never try to impose your beliefs, values, or points of view.
- Responding to the legitimate answers and manifestations of others. This includes returning calls, emails, and chats on social media where you are active.

Feelings And Expression

Do you want to be an assertive communicator? Rethink your feelings towards others and refine your speech. This means that you will adopt appropriate emotional stances and choose your words appropriately.

Here are some suggestions from my observations and inspirations gleaned from other good practical texts.[9,10]

The Need To Please Others

Stop compulsively trying to please other people. This is one of the key pieces of advice from Herbert Fensterheim's classic 1975 book, *Don't Say Yes When You Mean No: How Assertiveness Training Can Change Your Life*.[9] It is essential to learn to say no; otherwise, you will be a victim of all kinds of exploiters, and you will always be stressed and frustrated with yourself.

But try to say no in the right way to preserve the relationship. For example, a loved one who repays poorly borrows money. "Hey, Bill, can you lend me five thousand dollars until next month? I have to supplement the down payment on my new car." You could respond like this: "Yes, it could be, but I need to see if some of the money inflows I'm expecting will be confirmed. I'll take a look tonight and I'll give you an answer tomorrow."

If the friend insists, after receiving a clear and decisive negative response the next day, Bill will feel free to increase the tone of the negative. So Bill said no, but in a way that didn't create discomfort in the relationship.

Guilt Has No Value

Try to free yourself from any pathological guilt in your relationships. Otherwise, you will not be able to say no, to protect your rights, to set limits, and affirm your desires, needs and values. For example, some people feel guilty just for not buying a pair of shoes after asking the salesperson to show them some options. If you feel tormented by this type of irrational guilt, resolve it, even if you have to go to therapy to do so.

Try to identify your irrational guilt and its relationship to your nonassertive actions. Try to progressively control these feelings and act assertively.

You Are Never Wrong If...

You have to say what you want to say. At the same time, you want to create valuable relationships and know that what you say can make or break bridges. So look for ways to say things the right way. For example:

1. If you have good things to say about the other person, do so clearly and emphatically, even when you are in a conflicting situation.

For example, one of your neighbors is an engineer. He refuses to cooperate in a plan to improve the appearance of the building because he was injured. Also, three months ago, one of his ideas was not accepted by the other residents. You can say that if he doesn't agree, the plan will likely fail because he is one of the most active residents with good ideas and a superior technical qualification to manage renovations.

2. On the other hand, if you have not-so-pleasant things to say, you will never go wrong if you talk about yourself and not the interlocutor, that is, if you use "I" speech.

For example, your boss rudely criticized you in front of others and you asked to talk to him about it. Instead of saying that he was rude and inappropriate (accusation), you can say that you are upset about what happened and felt humiliated. You used an "I" speech. You are always right and beyond reproach when you talk about yourself. I mean, if you're talking about your own reality—experiences, feelings, values and attitudes—no one can blame you for accusing or misinterpreting them.

Stop Being Unjustifiable Bothered

If you are rushing down a street and a stranger suddenly asks for help because they are feeling dizzy and about to faint, it is human and ethical to do what you can to help. This help can hinder you a little, for example, by causing you to be late for work, miss the bus, or not reach the bank before it closes. But you did it for a good cause.

But if you're rushing down a street and someone stops you in your tracks to sell you something you don't want, you have the right to say no and avoid wasting time with the person. If the person is insistent, why should you accept this inconvenience? You do not need it. Do not accept being disturbed without a good reason.

Many people accept the inconvenience because they don't know how to deal with this type of situation. Here are some tips: Stop smiling and say, "No. Thank you," and move on.

If the person insists, use the "broken record" technique, which today could be renamed the "faulty robot" technique, which is as follows: Each time the person presents an argument or request, respond with the same message, e.g., in the case of the annoying salesperson: "No. Thank you" or, better, "I don't want this."

Never offer justifications when someone insists that you do something you don't want to. Justification weakens your refusal and opens the door to more insistence on the part of the interlocutor.

Don't Be Caught By Surprise

A colleague wants you to support a plan that you consider unfeasible. "Can I say you agreed?" he asks. You, wanting to please him, automatically respond: "Yes, let's go." Our brain is prepared to give socially desirable automatic responses.[11]

Automatic responses are motivated by impulses to avoid rejection or conflict, present a good image, and get rid of fear and other unpleasant emotions. The person who wants to be and speak assertively has to get rid of these problems. How do I do this? Here are some suggestions:

- Train yourself to pause briefly before responding. This creates space to assess the situation and consider a more assertive response.
- Use automatic positive phrases like, "Give me some time to see if I can add any ideas" or "I need some time to think." Simple and friendly, they politely indicate that you will not provide an immediate response and allow time for careful consideration.
- Consider that immediate acceptance can lead you to do unwanted things, but a negative response can eventually drive away good opportunities. So, how about waiting a little for

the creative options? Psychologist Edward de Bono, a respected researcher in the field of creativity, said that language puts us in the trap of double choice, where we just have to say yes or no. He suggests always considering an open option, rather than just yes or no, which would be the made-up word "po" (possible). So, instead of yes or no, you can be assertive by saying "po" and taking the time to think.[12]

Chapter Summary

This chapter explored the concept of assertiveness, a communication style that allows you to express yourself directly and honestly while respecting others. It contrasts assertiveness with passivity and aggression, highlighting the benefits of assertive communication:

- Increased self-esteem and confidence
- Improved communication and relationships
- Reduced stress and anxiety
- Improved ability to set boundaries
- Increased personal effectiveness

The chapter provides examples of assertive, passive, and aggressive behavior, along with tips for developing assertiveness:

- <u>Courage:</u> Accepting yourself and expressing your thoughts and feelings to others.

- <u>Respect:</u> Respecting yourself and others by listening attentively, using appropriate tone and style, and respecting boundaries.
- <u>Rethinking Sentiments:</u> Managing feelings like the need to please others and irrational guilt.
- <u>Using "I" language:</u> talking about yourself and your feelings rather than accusing others.
- <u>Avoiding Unnecessary Discomfort:</u> Learning to say "no" and avoiding being pressured into unwanted situations.
- <u>Overcoming Automatic Responses:</u> Pausing before responding, using phrases like "I need some time to think," and considering alternative options like "po" (a concept by Edward de Bono that suggests exploring possibilities beyond a simple yes or no).

Action Steps

<u>Functional Language</u>

What should I say assertively in situations X, Y, or Z? We can plan and practice assertive responses, to respond appropriately whenever the situation arises. Let's call this functional language.

Steps

1. Identify routine situations in which your assertiveness in responding is challenged.

2. Create standardized messages to respond to these situations. For example, a colleague often asks you for help with work that is not yours. You can prepare some automatic responses, such as "Yes. I'm waiting for a task from the boss and if time permits I'll help you", or "Yes, but maybe later I'll have to count on your help to share the work that I'll have to postpone to help you."
3. Test messages in real-life situations and use effective, automatic responses.

<u>Self-Respect Score</u>

How much do you respect yourself? It depends on the care you take with your language, the opinions you present, the consistency between what you say and what you do, and your readiness to respond appropriately to criticism. A person with a high self-respect score gets more respect from others and is more likely to be assertive.

Steps

1. Give yourself a score on a scale of 1 to 5 regarding self-respect.
2. Talk about it with a considerate friend and draw conclusions for your own development.

5

DO YOU HEAR BEYOND WORDS?

HOW TO DEEPEN YOUR ABILITY TO READ AND UNDERSTAND OTHERS' TRUE SELVES

J ames told me a true story that significantly impacted on him and transformed his communication with others. He and his son had a classic relationship between a rebellious teenager and a busy father with no time for his family. One day, during a usually quick breakfast, he looked at his son and said, "Wow, it finally looks like you have a beard!" The son replied: "I have had a beard for more than two months, but you never look at my face."

What do you think this suggests about the father's past conversations with his son? Do you think he is active in these conversations?

As a result of this event, my friend realized that he did not notice the existence of his son (and other people) and did not listen to him. He realized that many of his problems with his team members were caused by not observing them properly and poor listening habits. So he enlisted the help of an internal HR consultant at the company, and they identified why he wasn't listening effectively.

His behavior showed many of the classic barriers that communication experts identify in the listening process,[1] such as:

- Internal distractions, that is, concentration on one's own concerns, preoccupations, and worries.
- Planning responses while the other person speaks. This is due to the anxiety of speaking, defending one's opinions, making suggestions, and demonstrating knowledge.
- Selective listening: focusing on some specific information from the interlocutor while filtering other parts of the message. This is due to the privileged focus on one's own interests and problems.
- Emotional responses: reacting to the speaker's emotions rather than the content of the message. The reaction is often emotional as well.
- Cultural differences: misunderstandings due to variations in communication styles or nonverbal cues.
- The compulsive need to speak, transmit guidance, and present ideas and feelings of one's own.

James knew the importance of active listening, which is listening with full attention to the interlocutor, to deeply understand not only their words but their feelings, ideas, values. He has learned this in every training session since the beginning of his career. Despite this, did he know he was a terrible listener? Certainly not. We all mentally create an ideal image of ourselves. This positive self-image will go unchallenged except by traumatic events like a layoff or a phrase like "you never look at my face."

- If you want to be a really good listener, ask friends and colleagues how they rate you in this regard.

The HR consultant made another important point to my friend. He said: "It seems like it's not just about listening to people. The problem is that you can't see others, you interact with them but ignore them. You are trapped inside your private world and cannot look outside."

Active Listening – Foundation For Deep Understanding

Henry sees Liam once a month when he comes to load the truck. They talk about the task and exchange some quick ideas about things in life. Sufficient and good quality conversation, which makes everything go well, but there is no greater depth.

However, there are other types of conversations where deeper understanding is essential. Some types of relationships require understanding each other's points of view, building solid trust, strengthening collaboration, and creating meaningful connections that support personal growth and development. This is the case, for example, of the therapeutic process and management coaching, or of parents-children in family education. In these cases, active listening is essential.

Here are some active listening recommended practices:[2]

- Listen with full attention and interest. It includes providing enough time for adequate conversation, and temporarily setting aside other activities and concerns.
- Make a conscious effort to express receptivity, interest, and attention to the interlocutor. To do this, use verbal and non-verbal cues: nod your head, smile, and say things like "uh-huh"; it shows that you are following along.
- Do not interrupt the other person's speech except to add appropriate questions or encouraging comments.
- Listen to understand, don't respond: don't formulate your response while the other person is speaking. Focus on understanding your message.
- Don't be judgmental: avoid interrupting or criticizing. Create a safe space for them to share openly.
- Try to capture not only the meaning of the interlocutor's speech, but also their feelings.
- Ask clarifying questions: Open-ended questions encourage elaboration and ensure you understand their perspective.

- Summarize and reflect: Briefly paraphrase what you heard to confirm understanding and allow them to correct any misinterpretations.
- Ask for feedback on your messages. How did the interlocutor receive them? How did they impact the receiver?
- Consider that we all have mental filters, which prevent us from receiving all of the interlocutor's messages, and unconscious biases, which can distort what they are saying. Make a conscious effort to identify and control these obstacles to good understanding.
- Try to empathize with the interlocutor, understanding their situation, tuning into their emotions and ways of thinking.
- Maintain a courteous, disarmed and calm posture, whatever the message or tone of the interlocutor.

The True Empathy

Likewise, almost everyone knows, accepts and preaches the importance of empathy, but few people are able to get out of this abstract vision and practice real empathy for others. In the case of Henry and Liam and their sporadic dialogues when loading the truck, this does not cause any problems. However, if the relationship needs to reach a more complete and in-depth level of mutual understanding and become a path of growth for both, it is essential to reach a much higher level of empathy.

Here are some practical rules for this:[3,4,5]

- *Always put yourself in others' shoes.* Always do this before analyzing, interpreting, judging, giving guidance, or criticizing.
- *Develop and practice active listening.* We will discuss this below.
- *Talk to people from different situations and perspectives as an exercise to amplify your knowledge of them.* Instead of trying to convince them, try to understand their emotions, motives, ideas, and values. In this case, listening is much better than talking.
- *Read fiction and watch films.* Immersing yourself in stories can help you connect with characters, which can, in turn, help you better understand the people in your life.
- *Volunteer and help others.* Helping those in need can increase your compassion and understanding of different experiences.
- *Practice mindfulness.* Mindfulness meditation can help you become more aware of your own emotions, which can then lead to greater empathy for others.
- *Challenge your biases.* We all have biases. Be open to learning about different perspectives and challenging your assumptions.
- *Validate other people's feelings.* Acknowledge and accept other people's emotions, even if you don't necessarily share them.

- *Express your empathy.* Let people know you understand their feelings.
- *Be patient.* Developing empathy takes time and effort. Be patient with yourself and keep practicing these skills.

Much More Than Listening

As discussed in Chapter 2, active listening is much more than listening. However, we live in a world of information overload. People feel overwhelmed by the sheer volume of information and may have difficulty fully processing the speaker's message.[6] Listening to people and observing them can be difficult. My friend met with his son daily but could not see him effectively.

On the other hand, if we want to deeply touch another person, we must strive to make it visible; that is, we must illuminate the person.

How can I make myself and others visible? Effective behavior will achieve both objectives at the same time, as anyone who illuminates you acquires enormous importance in your life. So shine a light on people; like a mirror reflection, you will become highly visible to them.

Here are some simple yet effective suggestions on how to illuminate people and make you highly visible to them:

- Look deeply at other people, even if it's a brief interaction like saying "good morning." Your "good morning" should not be robotic and automatic.

- Observe people. If you say to a colleague, for example, "Blue looks good on you," they will be illuminated by your gaze. So, it will reiterate that they exist and you exist.
- Speak well of a person to third parties. Learn to admire other people's good qualities or achievements and mention them to others. For example, in a meeting, you tell people, "Let's ask Maria. Did you know that she conducted important research on this at university?"
- Ask questions that further bring out the value of the person. For example, "Nelson, you know how to cook; can you give me an idea of what to make for friends who come to my house for dinner?"
- Just actively listen to the person. They will feel important in your eyes and value you as a caring and wise person.
- Understand the person's feelings, concerns, and interests and mention them. A buyer from a client company calls to complain that the material has not arrived. You say, "Wow, this is a problem. People must be pressuring you. As a buyer, I know this is very stressful. I'll see what we can do to resolve this soon and get back to you with a solution."
- Include the person. For example, ask for the opinion of the person who is quietest and most neglected in

the meeting because they have a slightly lower status in relation to the other participants. At that moment, you illuminate the person and give them a voice. You have become very important to that person and have gained great visibility for them.

Chapter Summary

- Common barriers to effective listening are identified, including internal distractions, planned responses, selective listening, emotional responses, and the need to control the conversation.
- You have to "listen with your heart" and accept the importance of listening to gain a genuine connection.
- Good active listening practices are a necessary first step, but many people "know" them but do not practice them with the required level of awareness.
- The same can be said about empathy, a widely known concept but little practiced with due awareness.
- Self-awareness is crucial—we often have positive self-images that need to be challenged to recognize areas that need improvement.
- To be a good communicator, a person needs to overcome some challenges: The first is to effectively see other people; the second is to listen

to them effectively; Finally, you need to truly empathize with them, feel like they do, see how they see.

- To have real conversations, we need to relearn how to "look deeply" and see others. Making someone feel seen and valued promotes connection.

Action Steps

Your Active Listening Score

Are you a good, active listener? Test it.

1. See how many "yes" you give to the questions below:
2. Do you stop distracting your mind to fully concentrate on listening to your interlocutor?
3. Do you ask questions that clarify all points and show that you really want to understand the person?
4. Do you ask open-ended questions to inspire, capture, and value the interlocutor's opinion and points of view?
5. Do you deeply observe the non-verbal signals emitted by the interlocutor?
6. Do other sensible people agree with the answers you gave above?
7. Talk to wise colleagues about your ability as an active listener.

Test Your Attentiveness To Others

How effectively do you observe other people? Find out this through a simple test:

1. Choose a person from your relationship and list five of their best facial features.
2. Without the person noticing, check whether the characteristics you pointed out are correct.
3. Reflect on your level of observation and draw conclusions for self-development.

6

WHAT YOUR EYES (AND THOSE OF OTHERS) ARE SAYING

UNDERSTANDING HOW YOU LOOK AT YOUR AUDIENCE AND HOW THEY LOOK BACK IS A CRUCIAL PART OF THE CONVERSATION

Lena, 22, started as an intern at a large bank three months ago. Her supervisor, Mark, is a 50-year-old man who is conservative and not very open. He asked Lena to come to her office to discuss a procedure that she was not following with the necessary attention. She listened to his explanation with her head lowered and slightly turned to the right, her eyebrows raised, her eyes avoiding his, and a small, enigmatic smile, like she does whenever she is in a stressful situation. Just listening, no questions or observations.

Mark observed this same expression in three different situations. In the performance evaluation, he highlighted that she had an inadequate attitude, always keeping a deviant look towards his instructions.

Lena shared the boss's opinion with Christiane, who said: "Maybe he's right; I feel like you seem to have difficulty accepting authority and following rules." "That's absurd and unfair," Lena responded. "I'm not challenging anyone."

"It's not what you are doing, but how you appear to be," said the friend.

After talking a little more about the problem, Lena admitted that her facial expression, especially her eye contact, were disinterested and defiant. She wasn't challenging her boss, but she seemed to do so.

What would you do next if you were Lena?

Like our mayor, my father, in the first chapter, Lena bet on the right tool: dialogue. She asked for a meeting with her boss and said that she had identified her problem and asked for his help to change and grow as a professional.

Can Lena be blamed for her defiant look? Certainly not. She wasn't even aware of it. The way you look at others, or your facial expressions, is usually unplanned, but can always tell them something. They can sense that you are sad, happy, aggressive, calm, interested in talking, or not.

Like words within sentences, eye contact alone says nothing. However, we must pay close attention to it because, in the expressive set of the face, it is of great importance. Although we cannot fully control it, we can learn to present the visual contacts that best help us express the right emotions and postures to our interlocutors.

Functions And Complexity

Eye contact is one of the most important aspects of nonverbal communication. Through eye direction, movements, and dynamics, people gauge interest and open conversation, regulate turn-taking in dialog, convey emotions, and establish rapport.[1] At the same time, when contacting people from different cultures, sometimes without the resource of verbal language, eye contact increases reliance and permits the establishment of the first basis for cooperation.[2]

In daily life, eye contact functions as a silent indicator of power and status, intentions, qualities and defeats, interest, and respect.[3] This way, it plays an important role in the process of interaction, leading to sympathy, antipathy, cooperation, or competition. There is an assumption that mastering eye contact skills could increase power, persuasion, competence, and leadership. There is good and bad news about that.

The bad news is that mastering eye contact is quite a complex process, and its variables and the application of techniques based on them in everyday situations is nothing short of wishful thinking. The good news is that being aware of the important role eye contact plays in relationships and trying to instinctively read other people's eyes and control ours can improve our communication skills.

Common sense indicates that there is a gaze of a boss, a gaze of fear, a look of dishonesty, or insecurity. It also indicates that it is possible to learn to simulate these gazes, and the proof of this is the work of the actors. Good actors can scare us with a look of fury, move us with a look of love, and convey security and confidence with a look of leadership.

On the other hand, the attentive observer can read the clues given by the interlocutors' gaze and guide his speech accordingly. For example, a small sign of non-acceptance can lead us to seek feedback from the interlocutor. For example, I propose including two hours of fishing in a family trip that is being planned. My wife, my two kids, Judh and Cathy, and I gathered to talk about it one night. My wife and I realized in a millisecond that Judh is not sure that fishing is a good idea. His eyes tell us, without words, that he didn't like the suggestion. It doesn't hurt to ask for feedback: "So, Judh? What do you think of the idea?"

So, we have something to learn when it comes to eye contact.

Eye Contact For Better Communication

There are some practical behaviors we can adopt to better manage eye contact in our conversations. Here is a list of the most important ones, created based on my experience and references from practical texts and academic works:[1] [3] 4

- Maintain appropriate eye contact. This is generally considered a sign of attentiveness, engagement, and confidence. But be aware that prolonged or intense eye contact can be perceived as aggressive, intimidating, or even flirtatious, depending on the situation.
- Eye contact norms vary significantly across cultures, contexts, situations, and relationships. You will not have a manual or a checklist to use when the opportunity arises. So, learn by observation and develop your skills by training.
- Identify your ineffective eye contact behaviors, mainly those automatically triggered by negative emotions like fear, hate, insecurity, and lack of self-confidence. Substitute the inappropriate with appropriate eye contact. For example, instead of looking to the side or down while the other person is talking, try to learn to look directly into their eyes, in a "disarmed" and receptive way. This will make a big difference in the development of the relationship.
- Train to express positive feelings with your eyes —love, care, acceptance, happiness, calm, and trust in interlocutors. Make the necessary effort to convey warmth, approachability, and confidence in your eye contact.
- Be aware that prolonged or intense eye contact can be perceived as aggressive, intimidating, or even flirtatious, depending on the situation.

- In a conversation with multiple people, include everyone in your eye contact. If you are leading a meeting, instead of staring down and reading, look into their eyes, focusing on each one from time to time. If you are participating and a colleague speaks, try to look them in the eye as well. Eye contact shows that you are with the person in person, not just physically.
- Practice with a mirror or trusted friend, mainly if you've gotten feedback that your eye contact is flagrantly inappropriate, as Lena's. Be aware that bad eye contact habits can lead to problems in your career.

In Different Situations

Different environments and situations require specific visual contacts. Just like an artist who builds his expressions with reflection and training, we must also learn to work well with the grammar of the eyes. For example, a distracted look in the courtroom can turn jurors against the person, indicating that they are not taking your situation seriously enough.

Let's look at some ways to tune your gaze to different situations.

At a company meeting

- If you are leading the meeting, look each participant in the eye as you speak.
- Look carefully at whoever is speaking.

At a cocktail party or conference's coffee break

- Consider that eye contact between strangers indicates an openness to dialogue. Take the opportunity to make personal contacts and increase your network.
- Use eye contact as the first signal to approach the people you want to meet.

In a negotiation

- Be especially careful with the suspicious look because when you distrust people, they begin to distrust you.
- Also, be careful with an aggressive look, as it invites competition and makes it difficult to find win-win options, which should be the main objective of any agreement.
- Make the necessary effort to maintain a friendly and cooperative attitude.

Reading Others' Eyes And Microexpressions

We discussed Lena's case, but to be fair, we must ask about Mark's, her boss, role in the story. Don't you think he should be blamed in some way? Lena opted for personal transformation and growth, but, how about him? Didn't he have anything to change? Certainly. As a leader, he would benefit from learning to read the nonverbal expressions of his interlocutors better.

Had Mark looked at Lena's face carefully, he could have identified microexpressions that would have told him she was stressed. Had he noticed, he could have asked for feedback and taken the opportunity to be a real leader who coaches his employees in their development.

A look is crucial, but always combines with other cues, particularly facial microexpressions, which are brief, involuntary facial expressions that fleetingly appear (lasting less than a second) and reveal our true emotions, even when we try to conceal them. Developed by psychologist Paul Ekman, these expressions are considered universal, meaning they occur across cultures.[5]

Examples of microexpressions:

- Duchenne smile: A genuine smile involving both the eyes (crinkling at the corners) and the mouth, named after 19th-century French neuroanatomist Guillaume Duchenne, whose research helped us understand the link between facial expressions and emotions.[6]
- Lip purse: Compressed lips might indicate disapproval or suppressed anger.
- Brow furrow: Furrowed brows can signal confusion, concern, or frustration.
- Eye widening: Widened eyes can express surprise, fear, or interest.

So, if you want to be a better communicator, start paying attention to microexpressions, their combinations, and the emotions they reflect. While mastering microexpression recognition takes time and practice, the effort will pay off.

A good way to understand eye contact is to look at photos and films, focusing on the characters in their context. If we could photograph or film Lena's expression, what would we identify? We can never say anything with certainty based on facial expressions and appearance, but with good observation we can create very rough ideas about things. For example, in the Lena case:

- She listened to her boss's explanation with her head lowered and slightly turned to the right. I would say that she wanted to avoid discussing the subject, which could be interpreted as a rejection of her boss's instructions;
- Her eyebrows rose, which could be interpreted as a formal acceptance just to avoid punishment.
- Her eyes avoid his, an acknowledgment that he has more power.
- A small, enigmatic smile, which seems to indicate that she doesn't take him seriously.

Are these ideas correct? We can't say for sure. But, as Christianne said, "It's not what you are, but what you appear to be," and other people react to what we appear to be.

Chapter Summary

- Eye contact is one of the most important aspects of nonverbal communication. It is a quite complex process that depends on culture, context, situation, and personal experience.
- It is quite difficult to manage eye contact effectively and manipulate it with rationally established rules due to its complexity and the natural spontaneity of eye expressions.
- However, if the person is aware of the importance of eye contact and observes its functioning in interactions, it is possible to improve their skills in controlling their eye expressions and understanding those of others.
- It is also possible and desirable that the person learns by training to use their eyes to express themselves, avoid negative signs, and emit positive ones. Both negative and positive emotions are related to inadequate or adequate looks.
- If you look at others in a way that transmits good emotions, you will facilitate a lot of understanding and good rapport.
- It is possible and desirable that you learn by observation to read other people's eye contact in relation to facial microexpressions. This will enable you to better understand people and reach a higher level of empathy with them.

- Eye contact is also about active listening. It doesn't only suggest emotion, it also suggests that a person is listening to you.

Action Steps

<u>Look At Your Face</u>

Are your eyes projecting the emotions you want? Test it.

Steps

1. Identify five positive emotions you want to transmit to people through your eyes.
2. Ask someone to take pictures of you and clearly demonstrate each emotion in front of the photographer, with adequate clarity.
3. Analyze your photos and discuss them with the person.
4. Draw conclusions and plan to change.

<u>Reading Microexpressions</u>

Microexpressions always complement eye expressions; observing them to identify emotions is fundamental. Test your skills in reading them.

Steps

1. Try to identify microexpressions on a colleague's face when you are in a situation where you don't

have important things to pay attention to and he is distracted in conversation with other people.

2. Take note and talk to your colleague about your findings, trying to draw conclusions for your personal development.

7

LET YOUR BODY TALK

HOW TO USE NONVERBAL SIGNALS TO GIVE
STRENGTH AND COLOR TO YOUR IDEAS

P eople were told that a new supervisor would take over the next day. It was the delivery department of a dairy company, where 200 people worked in very basic functions such as moving products, picking orders, filling trucks, and delivering products around the region.

The workers were content with their jobs and resigned to the fact that there was no possibility of growth there. They were all anxious about the arrival of the new person in command, as they feared that changes could be introduced that would harm them. But at the same time, they were happy to be free from their previous boss, who always remained distant and didn't seem to care much about the people in the area.

At seven in the morning on the first day of work, Sue, the new supervisor, asked her assistant to call the four section leaders and tell them that she would visit each area to meet the staff. She began each visit in the area leader's office and then asked each one to accompany her to show her the area.

On the tour around each section, she, in a relaxed way, approached people who were working, exchanging ideas about their work, and asking about personal things, such as where people lived and whether they had been with the company for a long time. Before approaching, she looked friendly and after some time, she realized that they welcomed her.

Afterward, she agreed with the leaders to hold four sequential 30-minute breakfasts, which would be held in the cafeteria, starting the next day, with everyone from each sector. At these breakfasts, she spoke to the group for 10 minutes, with everyone seated, and then they went to the food table, where the conversation continued, with her circulating among the people.

Sue deserves an A+ in communication. From the point of view of nonverbal communication, she started in the right way. She did some high-impact things in this modality. Let's see:

- She went to each supervisor's area. This, in the most primitive terms in the repertoire of human instincts, is recognizing the supervisor's territory. Point for her. Do you prefer a boss who commands or one who doesn't take over your territory?

- During her visit she appeared calm and serene. This is what we want from someone who comes to bring order to chaos: power with serenity.
- She got close to people in their work, defining specific interests and values and creating intimacy.
- She hosted breakfasts, which, in our deepest emotional selves, equates to inviting people to her house.
- Finally, she ate with the people. Eating together is a celebration and assumes high symbolic power in creating belonging.

Two months later, one of the sector's leaders, Julianne, was talking to another, John. "It was really a good change for us," she said, "The moment she stood before me, I immediately knew she would be a great leader for us. She looked like a leader."

Territoriality And Personal Space

Sue's behavior is typical of great leaders. Sam Walton, the founder of Walmart, used to arrive by surprise at his stores throughout the United States.[1] This had a significant motivational impact on its employees. It also matches our species' most instinctive and structural behaviors, as indicated by Desmond Morris, a zoologist, ethnologist, and best-selling author.[2]

He argues that humans share a set of basic nonverbal signals, a "grammar" of body language, regardless of culture. Understanding these universal signals can improve your ability to communicate effectively across cultural barriers, although his book cautions against interpreting all behaviors through this lens.

Territorial behavior is one of the most primitive and basic forms of nonverbal expression. It has to do with ownership and protection of space, which results in personal affirmation both in leadership and in other occupational positions, in any profession. You won't communicate assertively if you don't respect your own space and that of other people. So keep an eye out for that.

What Do You Look Like

Remember what Julianne said about Sue? "The moment she stood before me, I immediately knew she would be a great leader for us." This good first impression remained throughout all the visits and encounters in the days that followed. First, she "looks like a leader," and she acts like a leader.

What do you think it means to look like a leader? It means emitting non-verbal signals that indicate legitimate power and the ability to obtain, to a certain extent, people's voluntary compliance.[3]

People appear competent, aggressive, generous, intelligent, unreliable, and all of these qualities are partly based in reality and partly based on nonverbal cues.

- What do you look like?
- What do you want to communicate with your body?

It is advisable to think about this and learn to manage non-verbal signals so that they convey the correct image of you.

Here are some examples of qualities and the nonverbal cues that indicate them:[4,5,6]

Power

Everyone needs it in proportion to the achievements they seek.

Examples of nonverbal signals:

- Occupation and defense of some territory; this means the land itself (especially in ancient times) or your desk in the office, your notebooks at school, your bedroom and privacy in the house.
- Body posture and facial expression of courage
- The intonation of the voice is firm and confident.

Security

Security in one's self ensures more respect. Insecurity attracts disrespect and abuse.

Examples of nonverbal signals security:

- A firm and clear voice
- Body stability (avoid repetitive anxious movements such as tapping your feet, pacing around, fidgeting, and many more)

Competence

If there is no competence, there are no opportunities in career and in life.

Examples of nonverbal signals of competence:

- Look carefully at the interlocutor.
- Make notes.

Responsibility

Having the essential quality in any work and in any relationship.

Examples of nonverbal signals:

- Maintaining your unwavering presence in crises.
- Attentiveness and readiness to act with ethical concerns.

Honesty

Using verbal and nonverbal messages consistent with the truth.

Examples of nonverbal signals:

- Spontaneous and easy expression
- Looking into the interlocutor in their eyes

Let Your Body Talk

Let us remind you of important points we have already discussed about nonverbal communication in chapters two, six, and this one so far: 1) Nonverbal communication is an essential part of interactions and often more important than words; 2) To be a good communicator, you need to be aware of the importance of nonverbal signals, strive to learn to read them in others, and manage them in your own messages.

Another important point is using gestures to reinforce your messages, which means letting your body speak. Research suggests that gestures are an ancient form of communication that coevolved with spoken language and have been used in conjunction for millennia.[7]

But, during the educational process over time, we learn to control verbal expressions and, especially, nonverbal ones. Gestures seem more "human" than words in communication, since the latter expresses rational and abstract things and the former expresses emotions. We learn and are afraid to use gestures too much, lest we appear primitive. As a result, we failed to make intelligent use of this resource which could greatly enhance our messages.

Do you want to be a better communicator? Free up some

of your body expression and make smart use of it to reinforce your messages. How do you do it?

Here are some suggestions on how to use gestures smartly:

- Assess how attached you are to gestures. You may find an exercise on this in our Action steps.
- Consider the type of communication you engage in most and what gestures could strengthen your messages. For example, do you teach? Do you make usiness presentations to clients? Do you guide people on excursions? What gestures could add expressiveness in the message you convey?
- Gradually free yourself from the psychological body ties that bind your body, such as the fear of appearing inappropriate or ugly; free up your gestures.
- If necessary, use a mirror or cell phone recording so you can review how you speak and use gestures in planned speeches.
- If you want to improve with guidance in this area, take courses on public speaking, body language, theater, or dance.
- To increase your gesture repertoire, look at good gesture dictionaries, observe movie and comic book characters and photos of important people, and try to identify valuable gestures for use.

Chapter Summary

- Recognize that anything that conveys messages without words—such as moving around in space, getting closer to people, and eating together— are important nonverbal communication tools. Use these resources wisely to reinforce your messages, whether you're in a leadership position or not.
- An adequate body posture indicates power, security, competence, responsibility, and honesty. Whether you are a leader or not, evaluate your body posture to eliminate vicious shapes and assume a winning position.
- Gestures are a natural and ancient form of communication that coevolved with spoken language. Over time, we learn to control them to the point of impoverishing our expressiveness. To improve your communication skills, freeing up your gestures and incorporating those that can reinforce your messages effectively and intelligently is important.

Action Steps

Assessing Your Courage To Express

How would you honestly evaluate yourself regarding the courage to express yourself with your body? Give yourself one point for each positive answer you give to the following questions:

Do you have the courage to:

1. Open your arms in the street to greet a friend you meet?
2. Clap for a good idea that a colleague presents in class?
3. Close your eyes and move your arms up while singing in church?
4. Dance a victory dance when the boss brings good news?
5. Pretend that you are crying with happiness (with humor) to say that you love the team.

Singing With Passion

People avoid releasing their gestures because they are afraid of looking ridiculous. Why not learn to be ridiculous and realize that no one in history has been killed by booing? This task is a bit difficult, but the results are worth it.

Steps

1. Go to a karaoke bar, preferably a crowded one.
2. Select a romantic song and sing it with passionate gestures, even if your voice is terrible.
3. If people boo, pretend they are applauding, and thank them emotionally.
4. Reflect and learn from the experience.

8

ASKING THE RIGHT QUESTIONS

HOW TO USE THOUGHTFUL QUESTIONS TO CLARIFY, CONNECT, AND INSPIRE

A large bank closed one of its branches in a city 100 kilometers from the capital. They wanted to give employees who agreed to be transferred to the capital the opportunity to keep their jobs. The branch manager was instructed to offer everyone the opportunity before the layoffs. So he started calling people to talk, and among them was Robert, my student, who narrated the case.

The manager told him: "Robert, I am transferring you to a branch in the capital." Robert found the sentence strange and said: "But I don't want to be transferred to the capital! My life and that of my family are all organized here." "Then I will be forced to fire you," the manager continued. Wow, this is pure blackmail!

Robert was perplexed and confused, especially because he and the manager had always had a very good collaborative relationship. The next day they talked again, and Robert realized that the manager's speech was not blackmail, but just senseless language caused by high stress. They decided that Robert would not go to the capital, as he had no interest, but would receive benefits that the bank was offering to those laid off, and the disagreement with the manager was also clarified.

If the manager had reversed the sentence, things would have been very different: "Robert, unfortunately, the branch is going to close, and I will have to fire all the staff, but I have instructions to transfer you to a branch in the capital, if you want." Now, everything makes sense and shows that the bank cares about its people and is willing to do things in the best way possible.

This short, true story shows us that a simple reversal in the order of information and questions can make the latter very inappropriate and, in this case, authoritarian.

Functions Of Questioning

Questions are a vital part of conversations, and, in their simplest functions, they can help people clarify situations and explain and solve problems. It is related to the operational purposes of the conversation, but the functions of questions go much further.[1]

Let's define that they perform four main, but not unique, functions: operational, investigative, inspirational, and rhetorical.

Main functions of questions

INSPIRATIONAL · · · INVESTIGATIVE

RHETORICAL ? OPERATIONAL

Operational Questions

Operational questions relate to the exchange of information to guide activities in social or work situations. For example, two people agree to meet each other at 2 pm. One asks,

"What time will you arrive? At 10 am, as usual?"

If the first person forgets to ask this (error 1) and the second person forgets to say that they will be there at 2pm (error 2), the result will be frustration, stress, and loss. Note that most disasters happen due to a combination of errors.

These questions are related only to carrying out day-to-day tasks. For example, "How many boxes of mayonnaise should I send this month?", "What was the income for May?", "Can you come by and pick me up on the way to school?"

By themselves, they do not bring emotion and are not related to deeper reflections. They are linked to simple and objective operations. But they can be very important at work, and mistakes can cost you your job. Therefore, it is advisable to ask the right questions, repeat and answer them as many times as necessary, and, most importantly, make a written record of them. It can be a simple text message, which will be remembered more easily.

Investigative Questions

People ask these questions when trying to understand more complex situations or processes and solve problems. Those questions push for more information, further clarification, deeper understanding. The complexity ranges from how to set up cable TV to scientific research into the trajectory of a comet. Most of the time, they are rational questions, even if they aim to elucidate emotional problems. For example, "How about increasing the advertising budget and using it entirely on our most successful products?", "Do you think wz1e might have problems with customers if we make a significant change to the restaurant's menu?"

Inspirational Questions

Inspirational questions are those with the potential to transform our lives. When I was 32, someone asked me, "Where do you want to be in ten years?" I remember that at that time, this question touched me deeply and made me stop and think. Questions like this can motivate people, inspire them to think, make them wonder, or consider different emotional perspectives. Examples: "Don't you think you deserve more in your life?", "What is the legacy you intend to leave?", "What is your purpose in life?"

"What is Man?" asked Socrates. "Man is his soul," he answered himself.[2] This is an inspiring question that makes us think about the foundations of our existence.

Rhetorical Questions

Rhetorical questions are those we ask without expecting any answer. They in themselves carry an indirect message, of praise, criticism, gratitude, confirmation. For example, "Nelson, are you my friend?", "What is life?" (at a wake), "Should we stand by while these mistakes occur?"

When used wisely, these types of questions can be an effective tool for reinforcing our messages. For example, shortly after announcing a promotion for Olivia, her boss asked her, with correct attitudes and nonverbal signals: "Do you think you will overcome this big challenge, Olivia? Of course, you will and I believe in you. Good luck!" In this case, the question carried a message of trust.

"Tell me, Peter, who was the winner of this month's sales?" asked Peter's colleague, knowing in advance that Peter was the winner. Just a question to please him. "Mary and I are dating." "Wow, don't tell me that? Are you kidding me? It is a wonderful surprise."

Rhetorical questions can be used effectively to strengthen your messages.

Do Not Forget To Ask Good Questions

Asking good questions is an essential part of the active listening process. If you're really paying full attention to the person, you'll pick up small verbal and nonverbal cues that should result in multipurpose questions. For example, you notice that when talking about a specific topic, the person changes emotionally. With due care, you should ask a question that will take the conversation to a deeper level. "Does this affect you emotionally, Jane? Do you want to talk about it?"

Good communicators get into the habit of asking the right questions for different situations and for different purposes. By doing so, they warm relationships and show other people that they notice and value them. As a result, they reap the highly positive feedback it brings.

Below are examples of questions we should never forget to ask people, derived from my own experience and good texts on the subject.[3,4,5,6]

Questions That Show You Notice And Is Genuinely Interested In The Person

If you observe the person's appearance, what they do, and what they say with genuine interest, you will naturally have good questions to ask. For example, you could ask:

- To a customer: Have you changed your glasses? They look great on you.

- To the receptionist at the doctor's office: "Beautiful handwriting. Did you take a calligraphy course?";
- To a gym buddy: "Long nails on your right hand? Do you play the guitar?"

If you are really interested in the person, you will naturally want to know what is going on in their life and doubts will arise spontaneously. For example,

- to a colleague from a previous job: "How are you at your new job, Noah?";
- to your neighbor: "Good to see you! What have you been up to lately?"

Questions That Show You Really Value The Person

People who develop friendly attitudes towards others have a genuine desire to value their presence. This leads to questions that open doors for relationships with strangers and also solidify existing relationships. For example:

- To a stranger on the street: "Hello, sir. Do you live in the neighborhood? Can you recommend a good restaurant that isn't overrun by tourists?";
- to a teacher friend: "I'm thinking about starting to give kids an allowance as soon as they're seven and eight. As an educator, what do you think about that, Ava?"

Questions That Express Recognition

Recognition, gratitude, support are examples of things that solidify relationships. Questions can indicate this. For example:

- To an acquaintance: "I've always admired your ability to talk to children, Mateo. Can you tell me more about how you developed it?";
- to a colleague: "That presentation you gave the other day was fantastic. What resources did you find most helpful in preparing it?";
- to a friend who is going through difficult times: "How can I better support you now?";
- to an employee: "You mentioned feeling overwhelmed. Would you like to talk about it?"

Questions To Improve The Mood Of People Who Are Down

Some questions have the power to lift people's spirits, moving them away from negative and distressing ideas. For example:

- To a friend: "Do you remember when you had that accident and were hospitalized for eight days, Sophia? You recovered much faster than the doctor predicted, and I bet your resilience will work efficiently again, don't you think?";
- for a son who is insecure about taking on a new course: "Have you ever stopped to think about how many tests you have taken successfully so far

in your school life? Why wouldn't you overcome this new challenge? I bet on you."

Bad Ways To Question

A person has just finished a complex task, and a colleague asks, "Why didn't you do it the XYZ way?" A good, ill-timed suggestion; it could have been considered as an alternative before the colleague started the task, right? These are the types of questions asked by Monday-morning quarterbacks or backseat drivers.

The following list of examples of bad questions was extracted from my own experience and good texts on the subject.[3] [4] [5] [6] We should avoid:

<u>Questions With Hidden Intent</u>

During a group project, someone asks, "So, does anyone have any ideas on how to approach this?" This appears to be a general investigation, but the person may be waiting for someone else to take the lead without revealing their own lack of preparation. This creates a misleading impression and makes open communication difficult. Others may hesitate to share ideas if they think someone already has a plan.

<u>Intimidating Critical Questions</u>

During a presentation, someone asks, "How can you justify such a weak argument with so little evidence?" in a harsh tone. This puts the presenter on the defensive and discourages him from elaborating on his points. It would be more productive to ask a clarifying question, such as "Can you elaborate on the data that supports your claim?"

Questions That Aim To Find Blame Rather Than Solutions

After a missed deadline, someone asks, "Whose fault is it?" This focuses on assigning blame rather than identifying the root cause of the problem and working towards a solution to prevent it from happening again.

Malicious Questions To Exclude Or Harm People

In a classroom, someone asks, "Why are you here if you're not good at this subject?" This question is intended to belittle and exclude someone from participation. It creates a hostile environment and discourages open learning.

Chapter Summary

- The four main functions of questions are operational, investigative, inspirational, and rhetorical. In every role, there are correct and incorrect ways of asking questions.
- Some inappropriate questions include those with hidden intentions, complex questions, or questions that aim to find blame.
- Good questions show people that you notice them, are interested in them, and value them.

- These days, characterized by polarization and emotional public scrutiny, it is advisable to be careful and ask appropriate questions to avoid misinterpretations.
- But you shouldn't be paralyzed by the fear of asking the right questions, as long as you don't have bad intentions, act with a clear conscience, and follow the rules recommended for the situation.

Action Steps

Receiving Questions Appropriately

You probably receive manipulative questions from others, often without realizing it. It is important to be aware of this and other malicious questions to prevent them from causing harm.

Steps

1. Be alert to identify a manipulative question in one of your subsequent conversations.
2. Once you identify it, analyze it carefully and discuss it with the person who asked it. Make sure they are an open and friendly person.
3. Repeat the exercise with other types of cruel questions.

Ask To Inspire

Questions are a tool to inspire people. Try to learn how to use this.

Steps

1. Think of an inspiring question you could ask a specific person in need of inspiration.
2. Ask the question and analyze the result.
3. Repeat the experience with other people.

9

ENLIGHTEN YOURSELF WITH THE CHARISMA CODE

UNLEASH YOUR INNER LIGHT, SHINE UPON YOUR AUDIENCE, AND STAND OUT IN THE RIGHT WAY

Five speakers were scheduled to speak to a group seeking to become entrepreneurs with small amounts of capital received from a nongovernmental organization (NGO). They were people with little education, who performed jobs such as cleaning streets, serving at gas stations, loading and unloading trucks, and domestic work. The speakers had very different profiles; with their high education and income, the group considered them "important people".

Three of the speakers spoke before the coffee break and communicated well with the group. They managed to convey clear messages, gaining the attention and interest of the group, which was very exciting. Soon after the coffee break, it was Mason's turn.

As soon as Mason started speaking he gained the group's attention and interest, but after 10 minutes of speaking things took on another dimension. People who were a little more withdrawn in the previous sessions began to speak up, laughter became frequent, people became more intensely involved in the activities, and many called Mason by his first name. The group laughed as they demonstrated knowledge of everyday things, such as the "bagged lunch", the accumulation of coupons, and the struggle to get a product on Black Friday.

At the end of the course, a small group formed around Mason, with excited people wanting more information or simply exchanging ideas with him. The last speaker and coordinator of the event, Charlotte, commented with good humor, "We are all good, but Mason has charisma."

What Is Charisma?

People say Mason has charisma. What does it mean? Do you know any charismatic people? Charisma is related to all we have been talking about—communication efficiency—but adds little ingredients that make a huge difference. Let's see.

The word charisma originates from ancient Greek and means "favor" or "gift" bestowed by the gods. In ancient Greek religion and philosophy, charisma referred to a divinely conferred special quality or power that endowed an individual with exceptional leadership abilities or prophetic skills.[1] A God-given gift. Can there be anything more desirable and important than this?

If it is a gift, then the person is born with it, right? In fact, it seems that some people are charismatic from birth, demonstrating exceptional talents for attracting and captivating others. Good for them! But, nowadays, it is known that charisma can be developed.

In modern psychology, charisma is viewed as a complex concept encompassing interpersonal skills that project a powerful and magnetic presence. Charismatic individuals are typically described as possessing attributes that allow them to inspire, influence, and captivate others.[2]

Instead of an inherent trait possessed by a lucky few, charisma is a collection of behaviors and attitudes that anyone can learn and develop. Olivia Fox Cabane posits this in the book *The Charisma Myth: How Anyone Can Master the Art and Science of Personal Magnetism.*

Cabane identifies three pillars of charisma: presence, warmth, and power.[3] Let's discuss them.

Presence

This refers to the ability to be fully engaged in the moment and project a confident and authentic self. It involves nonverbal cues such as strong posture, eye contact, and attentive listening.

Our speaker, Mason, is one hundred percent engaged. When he is in front of the group, he is completely focused on having a rewarding experience and getting his message across. He doesn't try to impress people, to appear intelligent, prosperous, and interesting. He is never afraid of people, so he speaks freely about his own life and the participant lives without fear of negative reactions. To each person, he appears as an equal who laughs at the banal things in life, such as brown-bag lunches, coupons, and Black Friday struggles.

<u>Warmth</u>

Charismatic individuals radiate warmth and approachability. They make others feel valued and respected through genuine smiles, open body language, and active listening.

Mason kept the participants engaged, asking their opinions, joking with them, answering their questions attentively, commenting, and listening to their comments about him or the topic. That's us!

<u>Power</u>

Charisma's power doesn't equate to dominance. In the context of charisma, it signifies the ability to inspire and influence others. This is achieved by clear communication, passionate delivery, and a strong sense of purpose.

Mason is an "important" person, but is also one of us. Therefore, his demonstrated knowledge and his mastery as a speaker can be of value to us, since he knows our problems and motivations. This way he is an example to be followed or applauded.

A Code Of Principles And Behaviors

According to Robin Sol Lieberman's book, *The Charisma Code: Communicating in A Language Beyond Words*, a set of principles or behaviors underlies charisma, a *code* that can be learned and put into action.

Lieberman argues that charisma is a "language beyond words,"a way of communicating that transcends spoken language. It's about nonverbal cues, energy, and emotional connection. It doesn't require grand gestures or an overwhelming personality but stems from authenticity and connection.

Here are some critical components of charisma according to the author:[4]

Cultural Awareness And Adaptation

Charismatic communication implies cultural awareness, that is, understanding and adapting your approach to different cultures. This means tuning your attention and your messages to the reality of each group–children, adults, businesspeople, workers, and priests. This way, you get to be "one of us," like what Mason did.

Energy

Charismatic people express energy and enthusiasm, a word that comes from Greek and originally meant "in god" or "full of god," suggesting you would likely radiate a brilliant light that enlightens and inspires everyone.[5]

You can cultivate and project positive energy, a key component of charisma.

We can easily observe Mason's pleasure in front of people. When he speaks, he is doing something that fulfills his mission of sharing knowledge. He puts his soul into it.

Trust

Charisma is based on trust. Charismatic personalities can establish a true psychological contract with people and deliver what people expect. They may feel like they are on your side and will put all their energy into doing what is in your best interest. We must be honest and transparent to maintain trust.

In Mason's case, it is immediately clear to people that he is one hundred percent committed to sharing all his knowledge and has no other hidden personal intentions in speaking. He is willing to share everything he knows with the class, without fear of being copied. He is genuinely interested in the students' difficulties, listens to them, and is by their side to do his job as a teacher to the best of his ability. This is easy to see. Have you ever attended a course where you felt the lecturer was holding back information? Trust is a very common quality that helps one to acquire charisma. Someone who holds back information is not on our side.

The Power Of Belief

Self-confidence and personal beliefs play an important role in cultivating charisma. Believing in yourself and your ideas promotes confidence and inspires others. Some questions demonstrate this principle: Can an atheist give a religious speech? Can a corrupt politician inspire honesty in people with his words?

Mason accepts his role as a speaker, believes in his abilities to do the job, and believes in the messages he conveys.

Sympathy, Reciprocity, Authority

In his book *Influence: The Psychology of Persuasion*, Robert Cialdini emphasizes the importance of ethical influence rather than manipulation, to build trust. The communicator's behaviors should be consistent with their ideas, transparent and aimed at producing positive results. Although Cialdini's book is aimed at marketing and sales activities, it provides a lot of relevant information about personal attractiveness and the ability to influence and captivate people.

There are three of the principles that Caldini presents that are directly related to building true charisma. Let's discuss them:[6]

Sympathy

Sympathy is the ability to attract and please people with nothing more than your presence. People want to be with you; they feel comfortable in your presence and like living with you.

Although it may be natural for some people, it is the result of behavior that can be controlled. For example, if you smile, you will immediately be more likable to others.

So, you can learn sympathy. Do you like being with people? If so, others will notice this and will tend to be happy to be with you. Are you genuinely interested in other people? If so, they will feel valuable in your eyes and value your presence. Do you experience pleasant feelings such as happiness, confidence, friendship, and calm? It's nice to be with people who express these positive emotions. If you don't feel these things naturally, be sure they can be learned through time. But you can do things that immediately lead to sympathy, such as smiling, being attentive to others, helping people.

Mason loves being with people. He usually looks at the positive side of each personality and creates a bridge of understanding based on common ideas, values, and feelings.

Reciprocity

We feel obligated to return favors or concessions received. If a person spontaneously gives you something of value, it creates a feeling of indebtedness. Now, can you imagine the value of a good idea for an entrepreneur, or good advice at the right time for a stressed person? Therefore, offers can come in the form of words in a conversation or speech. This is why some people say, "You changed my life with your words," to friends, speakers, and teachers.

So, if a person has a generous attitude and commits to sharing valuable things without withholding anything, there is usually reciprocity. Mason gives his best to the public and receives natural reciprocity through applause, nominations, and invitations.

<u>Authority</u>

According to Max Weber, authority is legitimate power. It is power that is accepted and justified by those who are subject to it.[7] Thus, authority can come from different sources, such as knowledge, experience, special skills, and position. If for some reason you are the head of the group and accepted by people, you have authority. That makes you special in some way. If you don't deceive people, then charisma can emerge.

People easily notice that Mason has not only possess the knowledge, but also experience in the subjects he talksHas about. As his speech flows, he refers to examples and cases experienced, which consolidates his authority.

What Do People Want?

What do teenagers want? What about older people? What motivates an accountant? We can say that people want things and differences between them will result in differences in needs and motivations. Charisma requires a good understanding of people's fundamental motivations. As Van Edwards postulates, captivating people is key to understanding what motivates them, and discovering their resource needs.[8]

The author points out that the fundamental desires that drive our behavior are the need for information, status, connection, certainty, autonomy, or justice. By recognizing the key resource needs of others, we can adapt our communication to resonate with them and build stronger relationships.

A Powerful Narrative

I was the presenter at a five-night course for a group that didn't have much access to such events. Some participants showed great motivation. At the end of the course, I gave a short speech thanking the participants and expressing best wishes for their success and future opportunities to interact. I ended with "Good luck to you all."

One of the participants was surprised by the clear and brief closure of my course and said, "No. It can't be just that, professor. Please tell us a few words!" I thought, "What should I say? What words does he want?" Fortunately, his request drastically changed how I understood the final messages given at seminars. They should not be brief closures like this, but an ultimate narrative of hope.

As Antonakis, Fenley, and Liechti note, a charismatic person is able to passionately present a memorable vision and narrative to people. So, three words are highlighted: vision, passion and narrative.[9] Let's discuss these three traits that the authors highlight as characteristics of charismatic people.

Vision

People want a positive vision for their future in any matter and situation, and a charismatic person can give it to them. For example, for entrepreneurship, a vision of correctly applying management principles and achieving success in business. Or for stress management, a vision of effectively organizing their lives and living more relaxed lives.

What do people want when they are interested in a specific subject? If you can provide them with a positive outlook, you will give them hope, one of the most desirable feelings.

Charismatic personalities cultivate hope and positive visions of the future even in difficult situations. It is not about denying possible difficulties but being prepared to fight and do your best, with hope, to overcome the challenges. That's usually what people want.

For anyone and in any situation, Mason has the best positive outlook possible. Even though people know the likelihood of failure is high in a challenge, they want a positive outlook.

Passion

Imagine two singers with equal vocal qualities. One interprets the songs in a technically competent version, with controlled emotions. The other releases all positive emotions into the interpretation–happiness, pleasure, love, and so on. The difference in performance is quite significant, in favor of the second singer. He puts passion into what he does.

We could say that passion activates all your positive emotions when doing something. A passionate person is enthusiastic and very excited about their works and accomplished acts.

Charismatic people tend to express emotions without fear which rubs off on others.

Narrative

Good stories can capture people's attention and convey or reinforce messages through education, inspiration, and emotional adjustment. You can learn to tell stories and refine your craft by practicing. Charismatic people are often good storytellers and can deliver memorable speeches that change other people's minds and lives.

Educational stories are those that make complex concepts or situations more easily understandable. A charismatic economist, for example, makes his subject interesting and clear to laymen; Likewise, charismatic lawyers, doctors, data scientists, and other professionals explain things in a way everyone understands. This makes a difference, because knowledge motivates—it is one of the most desirable goods.

Inspiring narratives show us how to overcome difficult situations, and what a positive future can look like. They show people who they can be in the future, resulting in the Pygmalion effect, that is, becoming the one you believe in and hope for.[10] Many charismatic people have a recognized ability to see who we can be and show us the way to do so.

Emotional adjustment is defined here as the combination of information and emotions in a way that creates psychological comfort and acceptance. Imagine, for example, a person who was abandoned by family members when he was a child and carries heavy trauma resulting from this. Suddenly, a mentor tells a story that presents the problem from a different but sensible angle, leading the person to a different perception of the event —a more comfortable and acceptable one. Charismatic individuals help people reframe their stories to build better self-esteem, acceptance, and worth.

Chapter Summary

This chapter explores the concept of charisma and how it can be developed. Here are the key takeaways:

- What is Charisma? Charisma is more than just being "important" or well-educated. It's a set of skills that project a powerful and magnetic presence.
- The Three Pillars of Charisma: According to Olivia Fox Cabane, charisma is built on three pillars: presence, warmth, and power.[3]
- Presence: This involves being fully engaged in the moment and projecting confidence through body language and eye contact.

- Warmth: Charismatic individuals radiate approachability and make others feel valued through genuine smiles and active listening.
- Power: Charismatic power doesn't equate to dominance; it's the ability to inspire and influence through clear communication, passion, and a strong sense of purpose.
- Charisma as a Code: Robin Sol Lieberman argues that charisma is a "code," a set of principles and behaviors that can be learned and applied. These principles include:[4]
- Cultural Awareness: Adapting your communication style to different audiences.
- Energy: Projecting positive and enthusiastic energy.
- Trustworthiness: Building trust through honesty and transparency.
- Belief in Yourself: Having confidence in yourself and your ideas inspires others.
- The chapter explores additional aspects that contribute to charisma:
- Sympathy: Being pleasant and making others feel comfortable around you.
- Reciprocity: Offering valuable ideas and knowledge freely.
- Authority: Demonstrating expertise and experience in your field.
- Understanding people's motivations: Tailoring your communication to resonate with audience needs.

- Vision, passion, and narrative: Presenting a clear and captivating vision for the future with passion and storytelling.
- Do you want to be a charismatic person? Imagine a charismatic person—his behavior, his attitudes in relation to others, and his body posture. Act as if you are that person. Never forget that action creates qualities.

The chapter concludes by emphasizing that charisma can be cultivated, and by understanding these principles, anyone can develop their unique brand of charisma.

Action Steps

Your Attendance Rate

How present are you in your tasks? Test it.

Steps

1. Define the three tasks you like most.
2. Rate your involvement in each of them on a scale of 1 to 5.
3. Think about your score and talk to considerate friends about it.
4. Determine how you can practice being more present in moments, situations, and conversations.

How Emotionally Generous Are You?

Do you struggle to give emotional gifts to others? Assess your level of emotional generosity.

Steps

1. Randomly choose three people from your relationships.
2. Evaluate your emotional generosity towards these people, on a scale of 1 to 5. Evaluate how much you give to these people in terms of greetings, compliments, thanks, and demonstrations of friendship and affection.
3. Discuss the result with a caring friend.

Your charisma is defined by other people. If you do valuable things to them, the reflect will return to you.

10

THE KEY TO EXCEL IN
UNDERSTANDING

DO MORE FOR YOUR CAREER AND LIFE WITH
THE ENTHUSIASTIC HELP OF OTHERS

Throughout life, experience and study indicate principles that we can adopt to improve communication—a process that lasts a lifetime. I define a principle of communication here as a concept or orientation that guides our behavior effectively following social dynamics. For instance, if you attack someone, that person might get back at you in some way, including through legal means.

Let's talk about some of the most important communication principles.

<u>Different Routes Lead To Understanding</u>

I was leaving the office when I noticed the receptionist, Karen, was silently crying. As the company had a very good, friendly atmosphere, I felt free to joke and ask an intimate question, "What does this mean!? Why would a beautiful girl cry?" She gave a small, sad smile and said,

"My father. We couldn't talk. His ideas and mine don't match. We always argue without agreement."

I had an insight into the situation and offered advice that could not cause any problems. I said to her, "Can I make a suggestion? I think it will work and resolve your situation with your father. But you have to promise that you will do what I recommend." "I will, I promise," she replied. Then I continued, "When you and your father start arguing, you will hug him and say, "Dad, I can't understand and accept your position, but I love you anyway." She hesitated and said: "He will push me; he will not accept my hug." I tried to convince her, "You have nothing to lose, right? Just do it. If he refuses your hug, well, you've done your part." "Okay. I'll try," she said,

The next morning, I found her smiling happily. "It worked. He was thrilled," she said.

What was the magic? It was changing the mode of communication. Instead of using the rational verbal mode, she used emotional body language. She will probably still not have a clear understanding with her father, but they will sustain their relationship on positive emotions. A new path of warm, intimate communication has been established, opening the doors to mutual understanding and acceptance.

The principle is: When things seem difficult, do not give up; use your creativity, change modes, and try new routes to achieve understanding.

A Message For Every Personality

To reach excellence in communication, one must consider the influence of personality on conversation dynamics. The American Psychological Association's glossary defines "personality" as "the enduring configuration of characteristics and behavior that comprises an individual's unique adjustment to life, including major traits, interests, drives, values, self-concept, abilities, and emotional patterns."[1]

Karen and her father were in an eternal argument, each trying to be accepted for their values. He was very conservative and thought that anything different from his ideas was "wrong" from his point of view. Would he change? It could be, but it's not likely. Will Karen change her values? Probably not either.

As Schwartz posits, in his article *An ecological theory of human values. (Journal of Personality and Social Psychology)* basic core values are relatively stable across the lifespan and resistant to change; His theory suggests that although specific behaviors associated with values may adapt to situations, the underlying values tend to be enduring.[2]

Karen and her father were in a vicious cycle: the more effort put into convincing each other, the higher their resistance, and the higher the wall is built between them. When they stopped the values discussion, everything changed for the better.

The principle here is that there is a communication strategy for any personality, including silence. In the case of Karen and her father, discussing value topics was not an appropriate strategy for their personalities.

Avoiding subjects and arguments can be a strategy appropriate for some situations. If it doesn't bring serious problems for the interlocutor and the relationship, it can be a good option, mainly in our days of radicalization.

Other strategies to fit personalities are the angle of focusing the subject, the length of conversation turns, the use of examples, and visual, auditive, or tact analogies. Some examples:

<u>People High In Openness</u>

Individuals high in openness are curious, imaginative, and intellectually engaged. They enjoy novelty, variety, and new experiences, in travel, hobbies, and learning new things. They are open to different ideas and perspectives and show a preference for intellectual stimulation and abstract concepts.[3] With them, you can explore all the angles of subjects, and space out to reach unexplored lands of knowledge with no fear of disagreement or discomfort.

<u>Low Agreeableness</u>

Individuals low in agreeableness are independent, assertive, and sometimes skeptical. They may prioritize their own goals and interests over social harmony. Normally, they are direct and honest in communication, even if it's blunt. They show a preference for competition and challenges and have difficulty compromising or following social norms.[4] Don't take their attacks as a personal offense. Maintain a diplomatic dialogue, and preserve friendship, even if the conversation is sometimes rough. Also, don't strive to convince them. Let it go, and go ahead.

High Neuroticism

Individuals high in neuroticism are prone to negative emotions, worry, and anxiety. They may be easily stressed or perceive situations as threatening. They show worry and ruminate over negative thoughts, are sensitive to criticism and rejection, and have difficulty coping with stress or uncertainty.[5] You have to offer them complete and clear pictures of the situation, with sound evidence, and you have to be attentive not to hurt them with criticism and comments. They will count on your positivity to feel comfortable.

Personality Biases

Personalities include biases that influence our thinking and our communication style. Peter Andrei's book *How Highly Effective People Speak* explores five key cognitive biases we should consider when communicating.[6]

Anchoring, for example, is the tendency to rely too heavily on the first piece of information presented. In communication, you can use anchoring to your advantage by setting the initial frame of reference. For example, mentioning your relevant experience upfront in a job interview can influence how the interviewer perceives your qualifications.

Another example is framing—a bias that highlights how information is presented influences our interpretation. You can frame your message in a positive or negative light to evoke different emotions and reactions. For instance, instead of saying, "You might fail this project," you could frame it as "This project is a great opportunity to learn and improve your skills."

Main Purpose Of Conversation

Another principle we can extract from Karen and her father's example is that the main purpose of the conversation is to promote understanding and not convince or change others against their values or interests.

The formation of values is a complex internal process that does not result solely from good arguments from interlocutors. Sometimes, we can and should, naturally, try to convince people, especially when they ask for opinions or need good ideas to avoid problems. But we are often unable to convince even a son or daughter, wife, husband, friend, or student.

So, good conversation should guide us to maintain a productive and happy relationship, even though we may have different ideas, sentiments, and interests. If we keep this in mind, we can unlock the key to more meaningful and engaging interactions.

You Don't Have To Talk

I heard an interesting story from a top executive. It will give us a third communication principle. In the words of that executive, he had two main characteristics: being constantly stressed and being considered antipathetic. He said he perceived those two phenomena unconsciously and could not understand the source of those evils.

One day, after a conversation with friends, he and his wife were walking toward the car when she suddenly commented on the finished meeting: "You know, you are not expected to give your opinion or guidance in everything. You don't have to talk!" He was struck by this comment, and understood that he always felt the need to express his opinion and to give advice, which made him stressed. He also appeared arrogant and antipathetic in others' eyes.

From here, we can extract a relevant principle: You don't have to be an expert out of context. If you are exchanging ideas between professional peers and discussing something relevant, then yes, it is the right context to present opinions and give advice according to your expertise. However, be attentive and do not act this way when it is not a requirement or an expectation of others.

Try to reach a reasonable balance, giving your opinion and advice when appropriate, and avoiding exaggeration in the role of an expert. Just hear and express yourself when you know it is expected.

Let Judges Judge

Why do judges exist? Because it is quite difficult to decide what is wrong or right in many of life's situations. Normally, there is good evidence to support both sides of each question. If someone becomes an informal self-nominated judge and pontificates on every little detail of other people's lives, they will become boring, at best, or undesirable in the most serious cases.

One crucial aspect of mindful conversation is not being judgmental. By suspending judgment, we create a safe space for both parties involved, allowing for deeper exploration of topics and fostering mutual respect. By recognizing each person as a potential source of knowledge and insight, we can expand our understanding of the world and venture into uncharted territories of empathy and connection.

Don't Expect To Live With Angels

People, including you, are what they are, nothing less, nothing more. They may have been different in the past and may be different in the future, but they are exactly what they are now. The problem is that we often expect other people to be better, much better, or even perfect—and in all these cases, disappointment will come.

People can disappoint us for various reasons: to obtain rewards, avoid punishment, or protect themselves or others. Deception is always a two-way process, since the recipient also plays a role in perceiving something as deceptive.[7]

Any rigidity in attitude toward protecting your ego or controlling others' behavior toward you will make communication difficult. For example, someone teases you because of an unconventional idea you expressed in a meeting. If you are a less mature person, you will react with resentment and hurt; if you are more mature, you will laugh with them, and that's all. After all, a small joke against you is not an offense and will not harm your purposes. Playing is part of good gregarious behavior.

Who do you think is better at communicating? Certainly, a mature person doesn't need to protect their self-esteem against triviality all the time. I guarantee that the person who expects too much from others would have no friends if they could hear what friends think or say in their absence. This does not mean that you will be an unassertive person, but that you will choose your battles.

The principle is to achieve excellence in conversation, create solid relationships for life, and cultivate flexibility and acceptance.

Chapter Summary

Communication Excellence Principles:

- Don't give up; explore new routes: When communication seems stuck, be creative and try different approaches to reach an understanding.
- Tailor your message: Consider personality types.

There's a communication strategy (including silence) for everyone.

- Focus on understanding, not winning: The goal is to connect, not necessarily convince. Respect differences in values and interests.
- Know when to stay quiet: Don't feel pressured to be the expert or always offer advice. Listen actively and speak when it adds value.
- Suspend judgment: Create a safe space for open communication by avoiding judgment and embracing diverse perspectives.
- Embrace imperfections: Accept people for who they are, flaws and all. Expecting perfection leads to disappointment. Be flexible and accepting.

Action Steps

<u>Deception Index</u>

Having realistic expectations about others makes your life and communications better. Evaluate your expectations.

Steps

1. Evaluate, on a scale of 1–5, how much you expect from others. If you expect them to achieve excellence, choose 5. If you do not expect more than the basics, choose 1. Choose a number that best fits your expectations.
2. Evaluate, on a scale of 1–5, how disappointed

you feel with people in general, with 1 being the least and 5 being highly disappointed.

3. Tabulate the result and talk about it with caring friends.

You Don't Need To Talk

Take the example of the executive presented in the session above ("You don't have to talk"). Inspired by it, evaluate your own compulsion to offer your opinion and advice.

Steps

1. How much do you need to talk, offer your opinion, and give advice? Evaluate it on a scale of 1-5.
2. Ask a caring, honest colleague if they agree with your score.
3. Talk with them about it.

CONCLUSION

A relative of mine (I'll call him Fred) had been an employee of a large bank for over thirty years, meaning he would retire in five years. The bank was in the process of cultural change and promoted a two-day seminar in which Fred was supposed to participate.

On the first day of the seminar, the speaker proposed that people participate in a group hug. Fred did not participate, due to shyness. He told me that he was quite stressed and out of control while people engaged in the dynamic, and for the rest of the day. At the end of the day, the speaker asked him to make an effort to participate in the next day.

Fred seriously considered resigning from the bank, to avoid participating in the dynamics. Do you believe that? If you have never met a person who suffers from social anxiety disorder,[1] this case seems unbelievable. Fred cannot change that for himself. To do it, he needs the help of a professional.

Apart from pathological cases that require help, personal change is very difficult, but most people can do it alone if they want. You have to reflect on some issues to make the necessary changes.

Do you want to be a better communicator or speak like an extrovert? Then do it—because no one can do it for you. If it's too difficult, try focusing on today's challenges: one small step at a time, better than yesterday, and striving to be better tomorrow.

Would you participate in a group hug at a seminar? If so, you are ready to free your body, gestures, facial and eye signals, and movements to achieve full expression. Do this and put energy into your messages. If not, return to a comfortable step that leads to this and begin a journey of change.

Do you enjoy being with people, including people who are really different from you and people with high maintenance needs? In this case, you will feel comfortable anytime, in any situation, and anywhere. Otherwise, be aware that emotions and feelings can be learned. Through study, conversation, and practice, you can learn to love some people, get along with most people, and diplomatically tolerate some. In general, you will be more prepared for happiness because the world we live in is full of people.

Are you ready to pay the price of change? You know that in communication, there are no wonderful scientific rules that will make you successful. It's usually more about what people already know, but often don't do, such as greeting the doorman, praising a colleague, recognizing and publicizing a person's merit, and smiling and greeting a stranger in the elevator.

Are you willing to face Alice, our friend from Chapter 1, who was dirty and nervous about the lack of water? To forgive a doctor who was rude? Perform a victory dance to celebrate the team's success? Knock on people's doors to sell a student development plan for primary school students, as my colleague of chapter 3? If you still can't and want to change, you'll have to make an effort to change some ways of thinking, feeling, and acting for the better, which is exactly learning.

Herman Hesse placed his own epigraph in his book, *Siddhartha*. The opening sentences are: "The bird fights its way out of the egg. The egg is the world. Who would be born must first destroy a world."[2] In a way, learning is modifying your previous beliefs, values, feelings, and behaviors and entering a new world, as a new being.

I hope I have contributed to your journey of becoming great communicators—like extroverts!

REFERENCES

Introduction

1. Mintzberg, H. (1990). The manager's job: Folklore and fact. *Harvard Business Review, 68*(2), 163-176.
2. Porter, M. E., & Nohria, N. (2018). How CEOs manage time. *Harvard Business Review, 96*(4), 49-56.

1. The Magic Of Conversation

1. Schegloff, E. A. (2007). Sequence organization of interactive behavior. In T. A. van Dijk (Ed.), *Discourse as social interaction,* (pp. 79-100). SAGE Publications. https://www.doi.org/10.1017/CBO9780511791208
2. Aristotle (2011). *Nicomachean ethics.* Translated by Bartlett, R. C.; Collins, S. D. Chicago: University of Chicago Press.
3. Scherer, K. R., & Ellsworth, P. C. (2007). Chapter 1: What are emotions and how can they be measured? In J. A. Keltner & J. T. Gross (Eds.), *Handbook of emotions* (3rd ed., pp. 1-29). Guilford Press. https://doi.org/10.1177/0539018405058216
4. Freud, S. (1966). *Studies on hysteria* (Standard Edition, Vol. 2). Hogarth Press. (Original work published 1895)
5. Sarbin, T. R. (1964). Role theory. In G. Lindzey & E. Aronson (Eds.), *The handbook of social psychology* (Vol. 1, pp. 223-258). Addison-Wesley.
6. Clark, H. H., & Brennan, S. E. (1991). Grounding in communication. In L. B. Resnick, J. M. Levine, & S. D. Teasley (Eds.), *Perspectives on socially shared cognition* (pp. 129-149). American Psychological Association. https://doi.org/10.1037/10096-006
7. Hanh, T. N. (2001). *Stepping into freedom: An introduction to Buddhist monastic training.* Parallax Press.
8. Covey, S. R. (2012). *The 7 habits of highly effective people: Powerful lessons in personal change (Anniversary ed.).* Free Press.
9. Siegel, D. J., & Germer, C. K. (2010). Mindfulness and interpersonal relationships: Toward an integration of mindfulness training and relationship science. *Perspectives on Psychological Science, 5*(4), 419-428).

2. Much More Than Beautiful, Right Words

1. Lasswell, H. D. (1948). The structure and function of communication in society. *Philosophy and Phenomenological Research, 8*(1), 111-119.
2. Knapp, M. L., & Hall, J. A. (2020). *Nonverbal communication in human interaction.* Wadsworth Cengage Learning. (Chapter 1: The Nature of Nonverbal Communication)
3. Attitude (psychology). (2024, June 14). In *Wikipedia.* https://en.wikipedia.org/wiki/Attitude_(psychology)
4. Infante, D. W., Rancer, A. S., & Conrad, C. L. (2014). *Building communication competence* (9th ed.). Wadsworth Cengage Learning. My Book
5. Moran, R. T., Harris, P. R., & Moran, S. V. (2010). *Managing cultural differences* (8th ed.). Routledge. https://www.doi.org/10.4324/9781856179249
6. Sue, D. W., Bingham, P., Poncé, A. R., & Rivera, D. W. (2019). *Microaggressions in everyday life: Race, gender, and sexual orientation.* Wiley.
7. Peterson, J. B. (2018). *12 rules for life: An antidote to chaos.* Random House Canada.
8. Bradberry, T., & Greaves, J. (2009). *Emotional intelligence 2.0.* TalentSmart.
9. Laird, P. W. (2014). *Pull: Networking and success since Benjamin Franklin.* Harvard University Press.
10. Milgram, S. (1967). The small world problem. *Psychology Today, 2*(1), 60-67.
11. Granovetter, M. S. (1973). The strength of weak ties. *American Journal of Sociology, 78*(6), 1360-1380.
12. Jankowiak-Siuda, K., Rymarczyk, K., & Grabowska, A. (2011). How we empathize with others: a neurobiological perspective. Medical science monitor: *International medical journal of experimental and clinical research, 17*(1), RA18–RA24. https://doi.org/10.12659/msm.881324
13. Knapp, M. L., & Hall, J. A. (2020). *Nonverbal communication in human interaction.* Wadsworth Cengage Learning.
14. Beebe, S. A., & Beebe, J. A. (2017). *Interpersonal communication: Relating to others.* Pearson.
15. Grant, H. (2021, December 21). How to become a better listener. *Harvard Business Review.* https://hbr.org/2021/12/how-to-become-a-better-listener

3. An Extrovert's Conversation Flow

1. Aristotle. (2000). *Nicomachean ethics* (T. Irwin, Trans.). Hackett Publishing Company. (Original work published c. 325 BCE), Book III, chapters 6-9
2. Goleman, D. (1995). *Emotional intelligence*. Bantam Books.
3. Schegloff, E. A. (2007). Sequence organization in interaction: A conversation analytic view. *Language in Society, 36*(1), 69-95. https://doi.org/10.1017/CBO9780511791208
4. Guynn, T. (2013, April 10). How to start a conversation with anyone, anywhere. *Forbes*. https://www.forbes.com/sites/michelleking/2022/01/05/how-to-talk-to-anyone/
5. Peabody, M. (2017, February 15). *7 powerful conversation starters that actually work*. Inc.com. https://www.inc.com/minda-zetlin/11-foolproof-ways-to-start-a-conversation-with-a-potential-customer.html
6. Bib48_MovieClips. (2020, January 12). The Godfather - Luca Brasi [Video]. *YouTube*. https://www.youtube.com/watch?v=oTpUWcpmAiI&ab_channel=Bib48_MovieClips
7. Rosenberg, M. B. (2003). *Nonviolent Communication: A language of life*. PuddleDancer Press.
8. Psychology Today (2019). *How not to be boring*. https://www.psychologytoday.com/us/articles/201910/how-to-not-be-boring
9. Swift, J. (1738). *A complete collection of genteel and ingenious conversation*. George Faulkner.

4. Assert Yourself!

1. Rathus, S. A., & Elias, J. W. (2016). *Understanding psychology* (10th ed.). Wadsworth Cengage Learning.
2. McBride, P. C., Trick, L., & Bacchiochi, S. (2017). *The effects of communication skills training on interpersonal communication skills and relationship satisfaction in couples*. Journal of Marital and Family Therapy, 43(2), 221-237.
3. Alberti, R. E., & Emmons, M. L. (1992). *Your perfect right: Assertive behavior for self-esteem*. Impact Publishers.
4. American Psychological Association. (2017). *Stress and health*. https://www.apa.org/topics/stress
5. Harter, S. (1999). The development of self-representations. In W. Damon & N. Eisenberg, *Handbook of child psychology* (5th edition, pp. 553-617). John Wiley & Sons, Inc.
6. Reale, G. (1983). *Storia della filosofia antica*. Vita e Pensiero.

7. Beck, A. T. (1976). *Cognitive therapy and the emotional disorders*. International Universities Press.

8. Rosenberg, M. (1965). *Society and the adolescent self-image*. Princeton University Press.

9. Fensterheim, H., & Baer, J. (1975). *Don't say yes when you want to say no: How assertiveness training can change your life*. Random House.

10. Murphy, J. (2019). *Assertiveness: How to Stand Up for Yourself and Still Win the Respect of Others*. Amazon Kindle Edition.

11. Baumeister, R. F., & Leary, M. R. (1995). The need to belong: Desire for interpersonal attachments as a fundamental human motivation. *Psychological Bulletin, 117*(3), 497-529. https://doi.org/10.1037/0033-2909.117.3.497

12. De Bono, E. (1990). *Lateral thinking: Creativity step by step*. HarperCollins Publishers.

5. Do You Hear Beyond Words?

1. Knapp, M. L., & Daly, J. A. (2020). *The interpersonal communication book*. Wadsworth Cengage Learning.

2. Grant, H. (2021, December 21). *How to become a better listener*. Harvard Business Review. https://hbr.org/2021/12/how-to-become-a-better-listener

3. Gillette, H. (2022, April 4). *How to be more empathetic*. PsychCentral. https://psychcentral.com/health/how-to-be-more-empathetic#how-to-act-empathetically

4. Miller, C. C. (2018). *How to be more empathetic*. The New York Times. https://www.nytimes.com/article/how-to-be-more-empathetic.html

5. Sobel, A. (2020). *Eight ways to improve your empathy* [Post]. LinkedIn. https://www.linkedin.com/pulse/nine-ways-improve-your-empathy-andrew-sobel

6. Infante, D. W., Rancer, A. S., & Andrews, P. A. (2014). *Building communication competence in a digital age* (9th ed.). McGraw-Hill Education.

6. What Your Eyes (And Those Of Others) Are Saying

1. Herrmann, A., & Thiel, C. M. (2007). The role of eye gaze in regulating turn taking in conversations: A systematized review of methods and findings. *Frontiers in Psychology*, 12, Article 616471

2. Hesketh, B. (1987). Seeing is believing: The primacy of visual cues in interracial communication. *The Journal of Social Psychology, 127*(2), 221-237.

3. Ifioque.com. (n.d.) *Eye contact types.* https://www.ifioque.com/nonverbal-communication/eye_contact

4. Ellsberg, M. (2010). *The Power of eye contact: Your secret for success in business, love, and life.* Harper Collins.

5. Ekman, P. (2003). *Emotions revealed: Recognizing faces and feelings to improve communication and emotional life.* Times Books.

6. Stanborough, R.C. (2019, June 29). *Smiling with your eyes: What exactly is a duchenne smile?* Healthline. https://www.healthline.com/health/duchenne-smile

7. Let Your Body Talk

1. Walton, S. (1993). *Sam Walton: Made in America.* Bantam Books.

2. Morris, D. (1991). *The naked ape: A zoologist's study of the human animal* (Revised edition). Random House.

3. Peterson, J. B. (2018). *12 rules for life: An antidote to chaos.* Random House Canada.

4. Eilam, D., & Corcoran, K. (2021, March 09). Threat detection: Behavioral practices in animals and humans. [Preprint]. *Neurosci Biobehav Rev. 2011 Mar, 35*(4):999-1006. https://www.doi.org/10.1016/j.neubiorev.2010.08.002

5. Davidson, B. M., Butler, S. M., Fernández-Juricic, E., Thornton, M. E., & Clayton, N. S. (2013). New perspectives in gaze sensitivity research. *Learning & Behavior, 41*(1), 116-136. https://link.springer.com/article/10.3758/s13420-015-0204-z

6. Tickle-Degnen, L., & Rosenfeld, L. B. (2017). The nonverbal communication of empathy. *Emotion Review, 9*(1), 3-14. https://doi.org/10.1146/annurev-psych-010418-103145

7. McNeill, D. (Ed.). (2010). Language and gesture. Cambridge University Press.

8. Asking The Right Questions

1. Ehrlich, S.; Freed, A. (2010). The function of questions in institutional discourse: An introduction. In *Why do you ask: The function of questions in institutional discourse.* Oxford University Press. https://www.doi.org/10.1093/acprof:oso/9780195306897.003.0001

2. Reale, G. (1983). *Storia della filosofia antica.* Vita e Pensiero.

3. Patterson, K., Grenny, J., McMillan, R., & Switzler, A. (2012). *Crucial conversations: Tools for talking when stakes are high*. McGraw-Hill Education.
4. Gallo, C. (2014). *Talk like TED: The 9 public-speaking secrets of the world's top minds*. St. Martin's Press.
5. Brooks, A. W., & John, L. K. (2018, May-June). How to ask great questions. *Harvard Business Review, 96*(3), 128-136. https://hbr.org/2018/05/the-surprising-power-of-questions
6. Atkinson, M., & Chois, R. (n.d.). *Flow: The core of coaching (The art & science of coaching book 3)* [Kindle Edition]. Marilyn Atkinson - Rae Chois.

9. Enlighten Yourself With The Charisma Code

1. Hornblower, S., Spawforth, A. & Duncan, E. E. (Eds.) (2012). Charisma. *The Oxford classical dictionary* (4th ed.). Oxford University Press.
2. [2] Van Edwards, V. (2016). *Captivate: The science of succeeding with people*. St. Martin's Press.
3. Cabane, O. F. (2012). *The charisma myth: How anyone can master the art and science of personal magnetism*. Penguin Books.
4. Lieberman, R. S. (2008). *The charisma code: Communicating in a language beyond words*. John Wiley & Sons.
5. Chrisma. https://en.wikipedia.org/wiki/Charisma
6. Cialdini, R. B. (2021). *Influence: The psychology of persuasion* (Revised ed.). HarperCollins.
7. Weber, M. (1978). *Economy and society: An outline of interpretive sociology* (G. Roth & C. Wittich, Trans.). University of California Press. (Original work published 1922).
8. Van Edwards, V. (2016). *Captivate: The science of succeeding with people*. St. Martin's Press.
9. Antonakis, J.; Fenley, M.; Liechti, S. Learning Charisma. Harvard Business Review. https://hbr.org/2012/06/learning-charisma-2
10. Pygmalion Effect. (2024, April 22). In *Wikipedia*. https://en.wikipedia.org/wiki/Pygmalion_effect

10. The Key To Excel In Understanding

1. American Psychological Association. (2018, April 19). Personality. In *APA dictionary of Psychology*. Retrieved June 10, 2024, from https://dictionary.apa.org/personality

2. Schwartz, S. H. (2012). An ecological theory of human values. *Journal of Personality and Social Psychology, 103*(6), 1086-1117. (https://www.emerald.com/insight/content/doi/10.1108/BJM-08-2020-0276/full/html)

3. McCrae, R. R., & Costa, P. T. (1999). A five-factor model of personality: The IPIP framework (International Personality Item Pool). *Journal of Personality and Assessment, 70*(2), 225-261.

4. John, O. P., & Srivastava, S. (1999). The Big Five taxonomy: History, measurement, and theoretical issues. *Handbook of personality: Theory and research, 2*(12), 102-138.

5. Clark, L. A., Watson, D., & Harkness, A. R. (1994). *The structured clinical interview for DSM-IV personality disorders (SCID-I or SCID-II).* Washington University Psychological Assessment Resources.

6. Andrei, P. D. (2020). *How highly effective people speak: How high performers use Psychology to influence with ease (Speak for success Book 1).* Independently published.

7. Buller, D. B., & Burgoon, J. K. (1996). Social deception theory: A theoretical and research review. *Communication Theory, 6*(1), 29-59.

Conclusion

1. American Psychiatric Association. (2022). Social Anxiety Disorder. *Diagnostic and statistical manual of mental disorders (5th ed.).* American Psychiatric Association. (https://psycnet.apa.org/record/2012-17357-027)

2. Hesse, H. (1951). Siddhartha: A novel (A. S. Weadock, Trans.). New Directions Publishing Corporation. (Original work published 1922)

DISCLAIMER

The information contained in this book and its components, is meant to serve as a comprehensive collection of strategies that the author of this book has done research about. Summaries, strategies, tips and tricks are only recommendations by the author, and reading this book will not guarantee that one's results will exactly mirror the author's results.

The author of this book has made all reasonable efforts to provide current and accurate information for the readers of this book. The author and their associates will not be held liable for any unintentional errors or omissions that may be found, and for damages arising from the use or misuse of the information presented in this book.

Readers should exercise their own judgment and discretion in interpreting and applying the information to their specific circumstances. This book is not intended to replace professional advice (especially medical advice, diagnosis, or treatment). Readers are encouraged to seek appropriate professional guidance for their individual needs.

The material in the book may include information by third parties. Third party materials comprise of opinions expressed by their owners. As such, the author of this book does not assume responsibility or liability for any third party material or opinions.

The publication of third party material does not constitute the author's guarantee of any information, products, services, or opinions contained within third party material. Use of third party material does not guarantee that your results will mirror our results. Publication of such third party material is simply a recommendation and expression of the author's own opinion of that material.

Whether because of the progression of the Internet, or the unforeseen changes in company policy and editorial submission guidelines, what is stated as fact at the time of this writing may become outdated or inapplicable later.

Social IQ Academy is committed to respecting copyright laws and intellectual property rights. We have taken reasonable measures to ensure that all quotes, diagrams, figures, images, tables, and other information used in this publication are either created by us, obtained with permission, or fall under fair use guidelines. However, if any copyright infringement has inadvertently occurred, please notify us promptly, providing sufficient details to identify the specific material in question. We will take immediate action to rectify the situation, which may include obtaining necessary permissions, making corrections, or removing the material in subsequent editions or reprints.

This book is copyright ©2024 by Social IQ Academy with all rights reserved. It is illegal to redistribute, copy, or create derivative works from this book whole or in parts. No parts of this report may be reproduced or retransmitted in any forms whatsoever without the written expressed and signed permission from the publisher.

Made in the USA
Las Vegas, NV
17 October 2024

97035314R00100